habit

habit

*The 95% of Behavior
Marketers Ignore*

Neale Martin

Vice President, Publisher: Tim Moore
Associate Publisher and Director of Marketing: Amy Neidlinger
Acquisitions Editor: Martha Cooley
Editorial Assistant: Pamela Boland
Development Editor: Russ Hall
Operations Manager: Gina Kanouse
Digital Marketing Manager: Julie Phifer
Assistant Marketing Manager: Megan Colvin
Marketing Assistant: Brandon Smith
Cover Designer: Alan Clements
Managing Editor: Kristy Hart
Project Editor: Meg Shaw
Copy Editor: Krista Hansing Editorial Services, Inc.
Proofreader: Water Crest Publishing
Indexer: Erika Millen
Senior Compositor: Gloria Schurick
Manufacturing Buyer: Dan Uhrig

FT Press offers excellent discounts on this book when ordered in quantity for bulk purchases
or special sales. For more information, please contact U.S. Corporate and Government Sales,
1-800-382-3419, corpsales@pearsontechgroup.com. For sales outside the U.S., please contact
International Sales at international@pearson.com.

Printed in the United States of America

First Printing June 2008

ISBN-10: 0-13-135795-6

ISBN-13: 978-0-13-135795-2

Pearson Education LTD.
Pearson Education Australia PTY, Limited.
Pearson Education Singapore, Pte. Ltd.
Pearson Education North Asia, Ltd.
Pearson Education Canada, Ltd.
Pearson Educatión de Mexico, S.A. de C.V.
Pearson Education—Japan
Pearson Education Malaysia, Pte. Ltd.

Library of Congress Cataloging-in-Publication Data

Martin, Neale, 1957-
  Habit : the 95% of behavior marketers ignore / Neale Martin.
    p. cm.
  ISBN 0-13-135795-6 (hardback : alk. paper) 1. Consumer behavior. 2.
Habit. 3. Change (Psychology) 4. Marketing—Psychological aspects. 5.
Marketing—Management. I. Title. II. Title: Behavior marketers ignore.
  HF5415.32.M375 2008
  658.8'342—dc22
                          2008006576

In memory of my parents, Ed and Mary Alice Martin

*"Such as are your habitual thoughts,
such also will be the character of your mind;
for the soul is dyed by the thoughts."*

Marcus Aurelius

Contents

Acknowledgments

Although only one author is listed on the cover, this book would not have been possible without the help and support of family, close friends, and old and new colleagues.

Kyle Morich served as researcher, editor, sounding board, critic, and cultural updater for the text. His advice to write the book like our conversations was the most valuable counsel I could have received.

Doug Rossier was my first corporate client to fully understand the implications of customers operating on unconscious habits. A senior manager at Sprint Nextel, he has become a relentless promoter of the habit framework across organizations.

Numerous experts across diverse fields provided the foundations for my understanding of the pervasive nature of habitual behavior. Any errors in interpretation or explanation are mine alone. Wendy Wood and David Neal, social psychologists at Duke University, were generous with their time and wisdom, explaining how habits trump intention in their experiments and in the real world. Jeff Quinn, a protégé of Wendy and David, was instrumental in pointing me in the right direction and providing ongoing critiques.

Russ Poldrack, cognitive psychologist at UCLA, provided not only extraordinary insights into the inner working of the mind, but also the limits of what is knowable using current technology. Similarly, Donald Norman of Northwestern shared his philosophies of product design and how the mind interacts with the world. His insights, shaped from decades of working with some of the world's most innovative companies, were essential to connecting theories of the mind with marketplace realities.

I was surprised and delighted to discover that the man who had started me on midlife career change, Dr. Naresh Malhotra of Georgia

Tech, had also become interested in the role of habitual behavior. He and Sung Kim of the University of Wisconsin (Madison) are examining how habits shape online behavior. They not only shared in their current research, but they also helped me develop a framework for my own research. I was also fortunate to be able to discuss the ideas of this book with Dr. Jagdish Sheth, one of the pioneers of customer behavior, my former employer, and a long-time friend.

Achala Srivasta took time out of her busy schedule to meet with me and explain how Nielsen Research is trying to uncover customer habits, a job much tougher than it sounds. She also shared many of the cross-cultural implications of habits from her years of global work experience. Harry West of Continuum Design and Harry Balzer of the NPD Group were also invaluable resources that gave me surprising insights that transcended their brief appearances in the book.

Karen Pryor, the noted animal behavioralist, helped me understand how the principles of dog training and habit training are essentially the same. She eloquently explained to me that positive reinforcement is not only the most effective, but also the most respectful way to work with people as well as animals.

Martha Cooley at Wharton Press/Financial Times saw the potential of the book and provided support from its earliest stages. Russ Hall provided encouragement, guidance, and feedback through the book's various iterations. My agents at InkWell Management, Richard Pine and Alexis Hurley, also helped guide me through the complexities of the publication process.

This book began with the smallest germ of an idea after watching my daughter Miranda use her cell phone while sitting by the cordless house phone. According to her logic, she should receive the entire credit for this project. However, it would have been impossible for me to neglect my business and other responsibilities for the two years it took to research and write *Habit* without the support of my wife, Diana.

About the Author

Neale Martin is the founder and CEO of Ntelec, Inc., a marketing, consulting, and education company. He has helped companies adjust their strategic marketing in the face of rapid technological change since 1995. For the past several years, he has worked on updating the principles of marketing in light of research from cognitive psychology and neuroscience that suggests that most of human behavior is under the sway of unconscious habits. Neale developed early insights into the power of habits as a counselor and program director for alcohol and drug addiction programs. After spending a year as a hospital administrator in Texas, he returned to school to earn his Ph.D. in marketing from the College of Management, Georgia Institute of Technology. Neale's insatiable curiosity across diverse subjects illuminates his work as he connects ideas and insights from science, technology, psychology, history, philosophy, and dog training. He lives in Marietta, Georgia, with his wife, Diana, his daughter, Miranda, and three border collies.

Introduction

This book reveals how two fundamental assumptions have led marketing onto a dead-end path: that customers are aware of what they are doing, and that they know why they do what they do. Using advanced technologies, neuroscientists and cognitive psychologists have recently discovered the counterintuitive fact that the unconscious mind controls up to 95% of behavior, so it is not surprising that the marketing theory taught for the past 50 years requires some serious updating. Managers and executives willing to revise their most cherished beliefs in light of this new understanding can gain the rarest kind of success, a sustainable competitive advantage.

Habit assists in this process by exploring the implications of the powerful but invisible habitual mind. By recognizing the influences of both executive and habitual mental processes, companies can develop products and services that are better for customers while simultaneously increasing customer retention and profitability. To accomplish this, companies must reassess not only their basic operating assumptions, but also their organizational structure.

Ultimately, *Habit* is about the limitations of marketing to perform its basic function: to help companies establish and maintain profitable relationships with customers. This failure does not occur because companies fail to follow the basic tenets of marketing—it occurs because they do follow them!

As a marketing professional, I must confess to having counseled my clients and taught my students the same rules of marketing that lead to such bleak results as an 80% new product failure rate and customers that defect even as they report being highly satisfied. Although I knew about these persistent failures, my sense was that companies were simply not doing a good job in execution, not that there was a problem with basic marketing principles. Because I passionately believed in a customer-centric focus, I accepted the articles of marketing on faith.

And as a true believer, I was unable to separate these dreadful results from the marketing models that created them. My faith in the underlying goals kept me from questioning marketing's most sacred cows even when evidence of their failures was pervasive.

Part I

The Force of Habit

1

How Habits Undermine Marketing

While driving to a meeting on the outskirts of Atlanta on a beautiful spring afternoon, I had the disconcerting experience of being unable to recall the last 10 miles of highway. Apparently, I had successfully navigated a 4,000-pound car at speeds in excess of 70 mph, responding to hundreds of cars around me, without any conscious control of my actions for at least ten minutes. This experience, familiar to most of us, illustrates the power and scope of the unconscious mind.

I was particularly aware of this phenomenon on a bright April day because I was on my way to a meeting with a client to discuss the pervasive role of habits in influencing customer behavior. This common example of driving on autopilot makes it easier to understand that we do the same thing in almost every phase of our waking life.

When we think of what it means to be human, we typically think of the attributes of our conscious mind—our ability to remember facts and faces, to solve complex problems, to create art and science. Indeed, our memories of the events of our lives create the sense of our personal identity. Yet for all the conscious mind's remarkable abilities, neurobiologists and cognitive psychologists contend that the unconscious mind controls as much as 95% of human behavior.[1] The conscious mind decides to go to a meeting—the unconscious mind drives the car.

---

[1] *Philosophy in the Flesh: The Embodied Mind and Its Challenge to Western Thought*, George Lakoff and Mark Johnson, Basic Books, 1999.

It seems counterintuitive that the massive amount of conscious processing power sitting atop our bodies should just be along for the ride. However, from an evolutionary perspective, significant benefits exist from just such an arrangement. This twin mechanism enabled our Serengeti ancestors to hunt for food without becoming food. Today these dual processors make it possible to talk on a cell phone while we drive.

Although multiple names have been given to the two distinct types of mental processing, in this book, we refer to the part of the brain where conscious cognitive processing occurs as the **executive mind**. We call the region of the brain responsible for unconscious processing the **habitual mind**.[2] The executive mind is where we consciously store and retrieve memories, create intentional thought, and logically solve problems. The executive mind can think about both the past and the future.

The habitual mind handles a vast array of functions, from regulating your heartbeat and body temperature, to storing thousands of responses to previously learned behaviors. The habitual mind is guided by the past but lives in the present.

Our understanding of the brain has been revolutionized in the past two decades. Through both clever laboratory experiments with animals and new technologies that enable us to look inside a working human brain, what we have learned during the last 20 years challenge much of what we thought we knew. Although these insights contradict basic assumptions in disciplines as divergent as psychiatry and economics, nowhere are the implications more profound than in marketing.

A quick review illustrates the point.

---

[2]   Giving names to structures and processes within the brain is somewhat arbitrary and risks giving the false impression that we really understand what we are naming. The executive and habitual minds are used largely as a convenience that reflects conventional understanding of these terms.

New Product Failure

Roughly 80% of all new products fail or dramatically underperform expectations. Although this metric varies between industries and services, the cumulative performance across all products and services represents a staggering indictment of marketing.

The plight of the Contour provides a good example of new product failure. In an effort to create a "world car," Ford Motor Company spent $6 billion to create a line that featured a compact model called the Contour, which debuted in 1995. The automotive press immediately validated the vehicle. *Car and Driver* put the Contour on its Top 10 list from 1995 to 1997. Edmund's named the Contour's SVT sporty edition its most-wanted sedan under $25,000 in 1999. Yet a scant five years after introduction, Ford killed the Contour due to a plunge in what had already been lackluster sales.

In another questionable move, Ford introduced two cars to take the place of the highly successful Taurus, which annually vied with the Honda Accord and Toyota Camry for the number one position in U.S. sales. The company replaced its perennial best-selling car with the Fusion, which is slightly smaller than the Taurus, and the 500, which is slightly larger. Combined sales for the two vehicles were a fraction of those for the Taurus at the height of its market domination. But rest assured that Ford went to exhaustive lengths in marketing research, focus group testing, and development of a multimillion-dollar ad campaign before it decided to replace its top-selling car. (By the end of 2007, the Ford 500 was transformed back into the Ford Taurus—only the nameplate was changed.)

One of the easiest jobs in the world is to criticize decisions that have yielded bad outcomes, and Ford certainly received its share of critical press. But the Detroit automaker is hardly unique. Thousands of new products and services are launched each year, yet only a handful will have any meaningful impact on a company's long-term profitability and survival. A prevailing attitude considers it impossible to predict with any accuracy which products will catch on with customers and which will be greeted with a shrug of indifference. Whenever people say "Let's throw a bunch of stuff on the wall and see what sticks," they are getting ready to waste a lot of money. It's hard to imagine any other area of business that would tolerate such dismal results.

Chapter 5, "Marketing from a Habitual Perspective," explains the source of customer apathy to most new product introductions, from television shows and movies to snack food and consumer electronics. At this point, it is important to understand that, for a product to succeed, it must first make a connection with existing concepts stored in the unconscious. The habitual minds of customers and potential customers must go through a physiological change to accommodate a new concept and a new brand. This is a process, not an event, and it cannot be successfully circumvented simply by spending money on advertising or getting good placements in stores.

Loss of Customers

Similar to the high cost of new product failure, losing existing customers is a chronic problem for most companies. Retention is critical for corporate profitability, but many companies routinely lose 20% of their customers a year, and better-performing organizations report losing 50% every five years. The cost of defections is harmful to both a company's top and bottom lines. The wireless industry provides an excellent example.

The cost of acquiring a wireless user in the United States averages between $300 and $450. That cost includes subsidizing handsets, paying distribution channel partners, running company-owned retail stores, and marketing. In the United States, the three leading wireless service providers have more than 175 million customers combined. Churn (industry-speak for the pace of customer defection) typically runs from 1% to 2% a month. If we take a middle figure of 1.5%, that represents a loss of more than 2.6 million customers a month, at a minimum replacement cost of $787 million monthly, or more than $9 billion annually.

The wireless industry also provides an excellent example of the profitability of keeping customers as long as possible. When those acquisition costs have been offset, wireless customers represent substantial margins because the incremental costs of voice and data services are very low.

But the wireless industry, similar to many others, has a long track record of treating noncustomers better than existing customers. In an effort to woo new customers, wireless providers traditionally give far better deals on phones and contracts to noncustomers than to those who have been with the company the longest. Only after an established customer defects do providers launch a "win back" campaign, in which they spend far more than what it would have cost them to keep the customer in the first place.

To hold on to customers, many companies have instituted expensive customer satisfaction and loyalty programs. Although these programs originally created a strategic advantage for pioneers—notably American Airlines and Marriott hotels—their very success has forced competitors to copy them. Now every major airline and most hotel chains offer significant rewards for frequent use. The same is true for grocery and other retail stores. What was once a major differentiator is now a costly requirement for doing business. These programs create spurious loyalty, at best.

Dissatisfaction with Customer Satisfaction

Billions of dollars are spent every year measuring and managing customer satisfaction. What could be more obvious than the need to create products and services that satisfy our customers? Many companies have customer satisfaction as a goal in their mission statements, and icon Philip Kotler puts the concept in his definition of marketing. The only problem is that customer satisfaction tells us almost nothing about what our customers will do in the future.

We return to this topic in Chapter 5, but at this point, suffice it to say that 85% of customers who defect report being satisfied or highly satisfied with the company they are leaving. In large-scale meta-analyses, satisfaction explains only 8% of repurchase. Having written my doctoral dissertation on the subject, this information was as dismaying to me as any marketing manager trying to figure out why satisfying customers isn't enough to keep them.

To illustrate this point, let's look at a company that is routinely criticized for making defective and frustrating products but that nonetheless dominates the world.

Why We're Addicted to Bill Gates

Each day, nearly one billion computers boot up with the familiar Windows or Vista icon. Even if we don't have the Microsoft operating system, most of us write with Microsoft Word, do math with Microsoft Excel, and could not imagine presenting without Microsoft Power-Point. No matter how much it might dismay us, we are all addicted to the software that Bill Gates foisted on the world 25 years ago.

Similar to most addicts, we no longer get a high from our addiction. But we can't seem to break the Microsoft habit. How did Gates get such a stranglehold on our lives?

He did not invent the original operating system for the PC or any of the productivity applications that made the desktop machine a staple for businesses around the world. And many of his customers complain openly and loudly about his products. The thousands of options that come bundled on every Microsoft application spawned the term *feature bloat*. And system administrators have their hands full trying to plug the seemingly endless flow of new security holes in Microsoft products.[3] So why is Bill Gates the richest man in the world?

The answer to this question is the reason for this book. Success does not come from getting to the marketplace first or from creating the best or cheapest product. Success comes from becoming the unconscious, habitual choice of your customers. Bill Gates is the richest man in the world because learning to use his company's software habitually became necessary to participate in the modern world.

Jonathan Lazarus, Vice President of Strategic Relations for Microsoft during the mid-1990s, sees the habit formation of early consumers being largely responsible for initial penetration of PCs into business markets. "IT managers couldn't keep PCs out," Lazarus says. "The corporate knee-jerk reaction was to reject the idea of allowing PCs in, but people had PCs at home that outperformed what they used at work." These early adopters bypassed IT by buying personal computers for their departments. "People built up habits at home," Lazarus points out, "and then asked, 'Why should my work life be any different?'"

In the early days of the PC revolution, most application developers were one-trick ponies, focusing their efforts on a specific product. VisiCalc and WordStar were pioneering products, but the companies developing them were narrowly focused. Gates understood the need to establish standard applications that end users would eventually use as habitually as they did a typewriter or calculator. His relentless quest to make sure that Microsoft was the standard resulted in a generation that thought Word, Excel, PowerPoint, and Outlook came with every PC.

---

[3] Gary Kildall is credited with writing the first PC operating system, CP/M. Seymour Rubenstein and Roby Barnaby are credited with writing WordStar, the first word-processing program. Dan Bricklin and Bob Frankston invented the first spreadsheet, VisiCalc. And Bob Gaskins and Dennis Austin created the first presentation software, Presenter, which became PowerPoint.

Lazarus sees Microsoft's entry into applications as key to the success of Windows. "There's no question whatsoever that having Windows applications was critical to our success," he says. "The user revolution becomes critical, and Microsoft changed the user expectation. By Windows 95, we totally captured user's habits, and by Windows 98, there was an absolute expectation of information at your fingertips."

For years, the technology community has debated the relative merits of Microsoft's products, often attributing the company's success to brutal business tactics. The truth is that a plethora of competitors existed at every stage of the PC revolution. IBM introduced OS/2 and bought Lotus in an attempt to wrest control of the software marketplace away from Microsoft. Apple's missteps during the 1990s are fodder for business cases. And a legion of software companies vied endlessly with the Redmond-based monolith.

The reality is that Bill Gates crafted his company's success by capturing the most important piece of real estate in the world: the part of our brain that controls our habits. And by doing so, he rapidly accelerated the information revolution.

Evolution and Revolution

The human mind evolved two types of mental processes to help our ancestors survive in a harsh and threatening environment: one unconscious, the other conscious. The unconscious, habitual mind is a cognitive strategy hardwired into humans as an evolutionary survival mechanism. Habit is the mind's way of handling routine decisions to free the newer, revolutionary, conscious mind for other tasks.

The habitual mind makes us cognitively efficient. It is meant to work *with* the executive mind, not in opposition to it. However, it is worth noting that habit literally has a mind of its own—habits are processed and stored in the brain separately from explicitly processed information. The executive mind cannot access the workings of the habitual mind. And this is why many marketing principles don't work.

Because we think the executive mind is in control, as if the habitual mind handles only mundane tasks, we grossly underestimate how much of our behavior is under the sway of our unconscious mind. Most of us find it hard to accept that the habitual mind controls 95% of our behavior. Yet think about almost any routine activity, such as walking on a crowded city street. We effortlessly process and react to hundreds of pieces of information—data that would overwhelm the limits of the executive mind. This is the norm, not the exception.

A useful metaphor is to think of these twin systems like the software that runs a computer. The unconscious mind is similar to an operating system, invisibly controlling the internal functions of the PC while simultaneously interacting with the surrounding environment (networks, printers, the Internet, and peripherals). The executive mind works similar to the applications, the programs that users interact with to accomplish their goals. Although we think of the application as the primary reason we use the computer, it relies on all the work the operating system is doing in the background. In addition, the application layer has a severe limitation—only one application can be active at a time.

This is the drawback of the executive mind, as well—it can think about only one thing at a time. The strength of the habitual mind is that it can process and react to hundreds of sensory inputs simultaneously without bothering the executive mind.

It's easy to think of the applications as creating the value of the PC, just as we think that all the important thinking takes place in the executive mind. But what good is that email you just wrote if you can't send it to someone? Similarly, to turn thought into action, the executive mind must hand off tasks to the habitual mind.

Marketers are similar to most PC users—great with executive applications, but at a loss when it comes to working with the unseen code controlling the machine.

The next chapter pulls back the curtain that veils the workings of the mind. Marketers and managers will be able to see how their current efforts work with or against the two minds of the customer.

2

You Are of Two Minds (At Least)

How do your marketing efforts interact with your customer's brain? Theories of consumer behavior were first articulated in the 1960s and were based on the prevailing psychological theories of that time. I was privileged to have worked with Dr. Jagdish Sheth for several years. Jag and his mentor, Professor John Howard, published the first book on consumer behavior. Cognitive psychology was in its infancy and MRI's were years away, so their theories were based on sketchy information, at best. But their work was highly influential and shaped much of marketing thought for decades. To understand marketing's successes and failures, we need to update our marketing ideas with what we now know about the brain's inner workings.

A quick look at the brain reveals pronounced anatomical structures, including four outer lobes divided neatly in two. But what is not obvious from looking at the brain is that two separate but interrelated systems evolved out of this complex and vast assemblage of neurons: the conscious and the unconscious minds.

Although we have long known that the unconscious mind controls autonomic functions, in the last few years, researchers have discovered that the unconscious also influences a wide range of highly complex behaviors. For example, a series of studies by Duke researchers showed that we do the same thing at the same time every day 45% of the time while thinking about something else.

The implications of this discovery are profound because our business assumptions are based on the idea that our customers are making conscious choices. Whether you are in consumer electronics, packaged foods, financial services, or business-to-business markets, most of your customers' behavior is the result of unconscious habits— yet most of your marketing dollars are spent trying to influence the conscious, executive mind. This might be news to you, but it's also news to your customer. Because the workings of the habitual mind are unconscious, the executive mind thinks it is in control of most of our behavior.

So when you ask customers, "Were you satisfied with your meal?" you set off an artificial thought process. The customer begins to consciously consider the temperature of his hamburger, the amount of salt on the french fries, and how long it took to get his food. And these thoughts, which weren't there until you asked the question, can alter future behavior. "Now that you mention it, I really prefer the french fries at the Burger Barn." And the next time that customer is looking for a quick place to get lunch, he might well choose the Burger Barn.

Similarly, when you ask customers why they shop at a particular store, you are catering to the executive mind under the illusion that it is in control. The simple act of asking the question makes the customer assume that this decision was conscious. The customer then makes up an answer that seems plausible. Market researchers diligently record this information, which becomes the foundation for marketing campaigns and new product development.

The litany of common business failures listed in Chapter 1, "How Habits Undermine Marketing" (high customer defections rates, new product flops, and the inability of customer satisfaction to predict repurchase), is largely a result of the habitual mind's influence. To better understand the real processes that govern customer behavior, it helps to understand how the executive and habitual minds work.

The Executive and Habitual Minds in Action

For all its remarkable abilities, the executive mind has the limitation of being able to consciously focus on only one thing at a time. The executive mind jealously guards this limited resource by turning over routine matters to the habitual mind, as with an executive handing off assignments to her assistant. If the mind has encountered and satisfactorily handled a situation before, it can write a script to automate the behavioral response in the future. If the mind perceives a situation as novel, the executive mind focuses on the problem.

Using the driving example from before, imagine that you are driving across town to a meeting. You are very familiar with all but the last couple miles of the journey, so you can multitask on the way there. You can talk on the phone, argue with talk radio, and even eat a quick lunch while driving in traffic. But the moment you get into unfamiliar territory, you stop all the other activities and focus your executive mind on getting you to the address. Novel situations activate and focus the executive mind.

This evolutionary adaptation works the same in the grocery store as it did in the jungle. Most shoppers follow the same route through the store, as if guided by an invisible track running underneath the floor. This frees the mind to focus on shopping, decide what's for supper, or ponder the mysteries of the universe. This strategy of efficiency carries over to shopping in most product categories where brands serve as cues to automate a purchase decision. The executive mind is constantly handing off decisions to the habitual mind in just this way.

Don't kid yourself: This behavior is not unique in the grocery store. This same dynamic occurs across sectors from airline travel to financial services. The executive and habitual minds are constantly interpreting and reacting to the environment in a complex and long-practiced dance. Marketing's greatest successes can be directly linked to aligning products and services with the habitual mind, whether on purpose or not. Coca-Cola's logo is so familiar that a customer can recognize it if only 5% of it is visible. The logo has not changed since Frank Robinson, Coke's first bookkeeper, christened the drink and also wrote the name in that distinctive script in 1885. The power of that cue has made Coke the most recognizable and valuable brand in the world.

Thinking of the executive brain as superior to the habitual brain is a mistake, just as it's a mistake to think of an executive as superior to a front-line employee. It's a matter of specialization and training. You might have to sell the executive mind, but you must win the habitual mind to keep a customer.

The power of the habitual mind has four significant implications:

1. Companies must focus on customer behavior, not attitudes or beliefs. Habits occur through the repetition of behavior and remain stable over time. Attitudes and beliefs are transitory and difficult to translate into predictable action.

2. Training the habitual mind is different than training the executive mind. Whereas the executive mind can learn through reason and intention, the habitual mind learns through cause and effect, reward and repetition.

3. To hold on to customers, you should keep them from consciously thinking about you. Though counterintuitive, automatic repurchase means the customer's habitual mind is in control. If the customer's executive mind is thinking about you, it could be thinking about your competitors as well.

4. To take a customer away from a competitor, you must break the customer's existing habits by first getting him to consciously think about the product. The stronger the existing habit, the more effort is necessary to dislodge it from an unconscious to a conscious process.

With these key concepts and their implications in mind, you are ready to explore in greater detail the role of specific brain functions and their corresponding impact on marketing. Ultimately, companies need to align their organizations to work with both their customers' executive and habitual minds.

You iDrive Me Crazy

Chris Bangle's assignment was daunting. The American-born car designer's task was not for the faint-hearted: to redesign BMW's flagship car, the 745i. Changing the iconic German car too radically would risk alienating the company's traditional customer base. Staying too conservative would stick BMW with a dated look for years to come.

In 2002, amid great fanfare, BMW rolled out the new 745i. Conservative it was not. Bangle's bold design generated an immediate and intense reaction from the automotive press. He was hailed as a genius by some and a madman by others. His design was praised and vilified, although far more of the latter than the former. The most dramatic feature of the car, its rounded trunk, was quickly labeled a "Bangle butt."

Many BMW customers were outraged. Stop Chris Bangle petitions appeared online. A few passionate loyalists even made death threats.

Like a performance-artist intent on getting a reaction, Bangle seemed to revel in the controversy. He described the car in terms of art and architecture, waxing rhapsodic about the ability to create three-dimensional effects in the sheet metal with five-axis milling. Listening to his passionate presentations, the designer comes across as either a genius or a huckster, or so full of himself that maybe even he doesn't know the difference.

However, BMW prides itself on engineering prowess, and here the new car impressed expert and enthusiast alike. The engine was more powerful, the handling was more precise, the braking distances were reduced—in every way, it epitomed the BMW. Traditionalists who couldn't appreciate Bangle's "art" could at least feel passion behind the wheel.

But one additional component that Bangle introduced on the retooled 745 made driving the car inordinately difficult and hopelessly frustrating. In a move even more controversial than the exterior design, BMW created an entirely new user interface (UI) for the car, inserting complex technology between the driver and the driving experience—the iDrive.

For driving purists, the notion that a car needed a UI might seem sacrilegious, but the burgeoning number of knobs, switches, and buttons used to interact with entertainment, climate, and navigation systems made the car cockpit resemble that of a jet fighter. So the design team at BMW, in conjunction with Microsoft and others, created the iDrive, a silver wheel that accessed eight sets of menus, allowing the driver to interact with more than 700 control functions. The solution was bold and ingenious—one dial replaced the disparate interfaces to create a clean, elegant alternative to the clutter.

The controller was positioned with ergonomic perfection on the center of the console so that the driver's hand naturally rested on the brushed aluminum wheel. Immersion Corporation embedded haptic technology (a trendy term meaning that the device communicates back to the user by applying force, vibrations, and motions) to provide feedback while entering commands. The menus also were color-coded for easier access.

Yet for all its engineering brilliance, actually using the iDrive was a lesson in frustration. "Technology run amok," one writer put it. "The 745 controls you through complexity," another wrote. This ultimate driving machine even came with an instruction card so valet drivers would know how to get it to a parking space.

My first exposure to the car left a lasting impression. The dark blue sedan pulled into the parking lot just as I was getting out of my car. A sharply dressed man in his mid-40s exited the glistening 745i and walked toward me. I asked him how he liked the car. "Want it?" was his two-word summary.

Ironically, at the heart of all this complexity was the desire to simplify. So how did a company with a history of engineering excellence fail so miserably at its stated goal? The central problem with the iDrive is that its creators designed a solution for the executive mind that should have been designed for the habitual mind.

We see this problem in interfaces as diverse as cell phones, remote controls, and web site layouts. This is a chronic source of frustration in everyday life as poorly designed products and services force us to consciously attend to tasks that are in the natural purview of the unconscious mind. But in the case of the iDrive, the design can endanger lives because drivers must take their eyes off the road to interact with the system.

Donald Norman, professor, author, consultant of design, and professional curmudgeon, acknowledges the challenges facing BMW's engineers. "They faced a difficult problem. The panel is getting progressively more cluttered. The iDrive is intelligently designed in the lab but doesn't take into account you're driving a car. They lost sight of the context."

Losing sight of the context is a pervasive problem created by the executive mind, which solves problems based on how the conscious mind works. Grouping the various functions a driver might need into nested menus based on a higher-order categorization schema is logical; unfortunately, the habitual mind doesn't work that way. Think of the unconscious mind as illiterate—clever, but totally nonverbal.

In this section, we prepare executives, managers, and marketers for an updating of marketing principles based on our current understanding of how the brain divvies up responsibilities between the conscious and unconscious minds. The creation of the first-generation iDrive illustrates what can happen, even to great companies, when designers and marketers don't grasp the importance of the habitual mind.

Your Customer's Two Minds

The human brain evolved so that we could survive the harsh existence on the African veldt. It did not evolve to shop. It was not designed for customer loyalty. And its mysteries cannot be divined through focus groups or customer surveys.

Although researchers have studied the brain for centuries, only in the last 20 years have they had access to its inner workings. Their findings provide clear indications where marketing theory has misguided us. Using advances in noninvasive brain-imaging technology such as functional magnetic resonance imaging (fMRI) and positron-emission topography (PET), it is possible to see the brain in action. But first we need to understand how different parts of the brain respond to marketing overtures.

Inside the 1500-cc cranial capacity of the skull sits 3 pounds of gray and white matter. This unassuming mass is arguably the most complex object in the cosmos. This is not mere human conceit. The human brain has roughly 100 billion neurons, each making an average 10,000 connections with other neurons. This represents a staggering quadrillion connections, a number greater than all of the known celestial bodies in the galaxy.[1]

---

[1]   R. Grant Steen, *The Evolving Brain* (Amherst, NY: Prometheus Books, 2007).

So how does this incredibly complex machine handle choosing a box of cereal from the hundreds on the grocery store shelf? How do we pick a financial consultant, a TV show, or a candy bar from the countless choices in virtually every category we can imagine?

Most of our beliefs about how we make such choices are based on a flawed model of how the brain works. Theories of buyer behavior, consumer choice, and customer satisfaction all rely on the idea that the conscious mind possesses almost complete knowledge of what we do and why we do it. An assumption also holds that our memories are accurate records of past events, as if the brain stores information on a hard drive. But like a navigator using bad charts, these mental models have led us far astray.

The reality is that most actions are the results of automatically executed scripts that have been encoded in the unconscious, habitual mind. Consumers often have little idea why they made a purchase, but they assume that their actions were conscious. So when asked, they figure they must have had a reason and craft what seems to be a logical answer. Marketers diligently collect this data and use it to create advertising messages, formulate distribution strategies, and design new products.

But what is really going on inside the customer's brain? How is it possible that the vast majority of behavior is not initiated by conscious consideration, but is instead the result of unconscious routines?

To gain some perspective, it is useful to remember that the fossil record indicates that our ancestors began walking upright roughly 4 million years ago, yet Homo sapiens have been around for only about 100,000 years. That's an eye blink in the evolutionary biological timescale.[2] Although we can't imagine what it would be like not to be consciously aware (because imagination takes consciousness),

---

[2]   A bizarre argument has been fomented between some in the religious and scientific communities that artificially pits people of faith against people of reason on the issue of evolution. The idea that evolution threatens God's existence is as invalid as the ancient church feeling threatened by a heliocentric solar system.

consciousness is believed to have emerged long after modern man was walking the planet.[3]

Philosophers and cognitive psychologists can struggle with the implications of unconscious humans, but for marketers and managers, the important point is that conscious thought is not required to successfully navigate complex environments. Sharks don't remember whether they have been to a particular cove before, nor do bees recognize whether they have visited a specific flower. But they are able to execute complex behaviors in response to cues and internal states. And they are able to learn.

As the human brain evolved, it developed a conscious mind as a complement to the unconscious mind.[4] The unconscious human mind could craft complex reactions to the environment, while the new conscious mind could remember intentionally and could plan. In other words, humans became aware of the past and the future. The conscious mind also developed an awareness of self.

Let's pop the hood and take a look at how the brain's architecture created such an odd couple of minds.

A Quick Tour of the Brain

Numerous excellent books detail the complexity of the human brain based on breakthrough research from the past two decades. This is not one of them. Our goal is to extract and simplify the current understanding of how our brains work and then rapidly apply those insights to every element of customer interaction with products and services, brands and advertising, distribution channels, and warranties.

---

[3] By "conscious," we refer to specific kinds of mental processes that involve self-awareness.

[4] Significant debate swirls about how many "minds" humans possess, based largely on different memory systems that have been identified.

Depending on how you view it, the brain tells different stories.

Viewed from the side, the brain looks like a house built without a master plan, one that was haphazardly added on to over the years. Although we identify "humanness" strongly with the most recent addition, the **cerebrum**, this region of the brain rests squarely on its predecessor, the **limbic system**, which houses the emotional parts of the brain, the **amygdala**, as well as the central switchboards of the **hippocampus** and the **basal ganglia**. The cerebrum and the limbic system rest on the **hindbrain**, the brain's basement that contains the **cerebellum** and the **brain stem**. These are the only parts of the brain we need to remember.

Don't let these names intimidate you: *Hippocampus* is Greek for "seahorse" and *amygdala* is Latin for "almond." *Cerebrum* is Latin for "brain," and *cerebellum* is Latin for "little brain." These structures will serve as landmarks as we navigate.

Viewed from the front, the brain appears divided into seemingly identical halves, with dense fibrous threads connecting the two hemispheres. Roughly equivalent in appearance, the two sides have divvied up some basic chores: Typically, the right side of the brain dominates for spatial abilities and visual imagery, while the left side handles language, mathematical calculations, and logical abilities.

Viewed with increasing magnification, the brain's story changes dramatically. The lobes, fissures, and wrinkles give way to an incredible tangle of tiny neurons interconnecting via skinny axons and dendrites, like alien spiders spinning fanciful webs. Thinking of the various structures of the brain as being responsible for specific functions is tempting, but each section is richly connected to the others through this web of neurons, as is the brain to the rest of the body.

By continuing the magnification process, we see that the axons and dendrites fall just short of touching, creating what is called the synaptic cleft. The landscape at this level of magnification reveals a remarkable communications network. At the end of an axon are vesicles filled with chemical messengers, called neurotransmitters. On the other side of the gap are tiny gateways that respond specifically to the neurotransmitter from the axon. An electrical pulse causes the release of these chemicals, completing the circuit that conveys messages from throughout the body and across the billions of interconnected neurons in the brain.

We might like to avoid discussions of neurology, but ultimately the relationships between an axon's neurotransmitters and the dendrite's gateways determine the success or failure of any marketing effort. But don't panic—we minimize the use of biological terms, and there will be no tests.

All that we are, all that we think and imagine, and all that we do emerges from this ungainly arrangement of neurons packed densely inside our skulls. But to understand the idea of multiple minds, we need to view the brain from one other perspective: through the lens of time.

The Dinosaur Brain[5]

Let's return to the side view of the brain. The brain evolved from the bottom up. The farther down we go, the further back in time we reach. We can conveniently think of the brain in three sections: the hindbrain, the limbic system, and the cerebral cortex.

The hindbrain sits at the base of the skull and includes three important structures: the pons, medulla oblongata, and cerebellum. From an evolutionary perspective, the roots of these structures date back 200 million years, as their shapes are evident in fossilized dinosaur skulls. Because of this, neurophysiologists have dubbed this area in humans the "dinosaur brain."

Having a dinosaur brain is far from an insult. Dinosaurs dominated the global landscape for 135 million years, displaying a remarkable ability to adapt, survive, and thrive. (In contrast, humans began

---

[5] From R. Grant Steen's excellent book, *The Evolving Brain*.

to migrate from Africa only 60,000 years ago.) It is the nature of evolution to preserve that which works well, retasking existing structures to solve novel problems. That we have the same mechanism built into our brains that worked so well for the dinosaur is important for marketers to understand because it provides a model of how humans interact with the environment. Much of buyer behavior taps into the dinosaur brain.

Before we conjure up images of Velociraptors shopping at the mall, the important contributions of the dinosaur brain are autonomic and integrative processes. Autonomic processes are the myriad functions the brain controls that keep us alive without conscious intervention, such as maintaining the correct level of acidity in our blood and digesting food. Although we have long known that the dinosaur brain controlled these functions, we have only recently uncovered the extent of the integrative functions, including important components of learning.

The cerebellum, in particular, plays a critical role in how users interact with products. The cerebellum has long been known to play an important role in how we move through the world. This region of the brain constantly monitors what you mean to do and what you are really doing as you interact with the environment, attempting to harmonize intention and action. Learning to use a new cell phone or game system largely involves training the cerebellum. The relentless advance of technologically sophisticated products all too often fails to take into account the role of the dinosaur brain.

We can see an example of the importance of the cerebellum in the deceptively complex task of walking smoothly. Walking is a series of controlled falls. We balance on one leg and then throw our weight forward, thrusting our opposite leg ahead to keep our faces from smacking the ground. Giovanni Cavagna, professor of physiology at the University of Milan, has studied walking for decades. He describes the upright locomotion of humans as an inverted pendulum. We walk by pivoting on one foot while swinging the other in an arc, shifting between maximum kinetic and potential energy. Although the physics are inordinately complex, we carry out this movement every day unconsciously, thanks in large part to our cerebellum.

You can perform an experiment on your own to validate the usefulness of the cerebellum in controlling movement. Run down a long flight of stairs as fast as you can. At the halfway point, look down without changing pace. After you pick yourself up from the bottom of the stairs and check for broken bones, you will have developed a better appreciation for your cerebellum. Your executive brain cannot execute the inordinately complicated coordination of body parts that the dinosaur brain controls effortlessly.

But these abilities are not inborn. The cerebellum learns from experience. I had a recent opportunity to experience this process firsthand at a family reunion.

My brother brought a game to the Martin reunion that most of us were unfamiliar with—a hyper-competition-inducing number called Corn Hole. Two platforms 2 feet wide and 4 feet long are positioned 30 feet apart. The boards are elevated and slanted upward as you face them, and both boards have a hole toward the top. The object of the game is to stand by one of the boards and toss a bag filled with corn across the 30-foot gap so that it lands and stays on the board (1 point) or goes into the hole (3 points). The first person (or team) to score 21 points wins.

Watching someone new to the game throw the first couple of beanbags provided an excellent window into how the conscious and unconscious minds work together. The executive mind quickly grasps the rules of the game and devises a strategy to make the first throw. However, the conscious motor coordination fails to produce good results. Most initial throws miss the board completely. Those that hit the board slide off, scoring no points. However, by the second or third game, most players' cerebellums had acquired enough experience to guide the throws. They started hitting the board with consistency, and by the end of the day, they were routinely tossing the bags 30 feet into the small holes at the top of the board.

W. T. Thach and J. G. Keating of Washington University School of Medicine in St. Louis, Missouri, have studied the amazing properties of the cerebellum to guide complex movements and adapt to changing conditions. They devised experiments in which subjects wore prismatic spectacles that distorted their vision. The subjects then attempted to throw objects (clay balls or darts) at a target. With practice, subjects' accuracy rapidly approximated their skill level without vision distortion. All the muscle and joint coordination quickly and automatically adapted based on the new visual feedback mechanisms. To the cerebellum, at least, perception is reality.

With this insight, let's return to the iDrive example. Viewed from the perspective of the dinosaur brain, the problems with the iDrive become immediately apparent. Most of driving a car is done unconsciously. As with walking, we don't consciously think about sending messages to the muscles. The amount of pressure applied to the gas pedal and the force put on the steering wheel are constantly changing based on feedback from our eyes and other senses. The cerebellum fine-tunes our movements, so developing the coordination to hit the tiny buttons to change the radio station or turn on the heater can be incorporated into its circuitry with minimal effect on our driving.

However, the original iDrive system, with its eight compass points and nested menus, did not provide the feedback mechanisms necessary to train the cerebellum. Engineers at BMW thought they had solved the problem by using colored menus and tactile feedback, but the logic of the iDrive is the logic of the executive mind, the *cerebrum*. The executive mind comprehends choices in virtual space. The dinosaur brain can't even understand the concept of virtual space.

Interestingly, Bangle's "bold new design" has become mainstream, the once radical lines now clearly visible on Japanese and Korean imitators. But the dinosaur brain could not adapt to the complexity of the original user interface. The second generation of the iDrive cut the number of functions in half. Although it still requires a steep learning curve, the new system accommodates the need for a UI to integrate the disparate systems in the modern automobile without detracting from the car's primary job: to carry you wherever your executive mind decides to go.

Designing for the Dinosaur Brain

The pervasiveness of the product complexity problem is obvious in this all too familiar example. Answering my mobile phone while on an extended business trip, I was greeted by my wife's voice nearly in tears. "There are seven remotes in the living room! Seven! I just want to watch television." At first I was amused by my normally competent wife's inability to pick up the cable remote and hit the All On button. But that rush of geeky superiority was quickly replaced by a marketer's complete frustration with companies that foist poorly thought-out user interfaces on an unsuspecting population.

My wife was confronted by remotes for the TV, stereo receiver, DVD player, DVR, digital cable box, and VCR—and a $450 "universal remote." Each remote had 30 to 45 buttons, no common approach for handling the same task, and a wide variety of layouts. My ability to distinguish which device performed which function at a glance was partly a byproduct of a Ph.D. from an engineering school, but more an indicator of how tolerant I had become of poorly designed and overly complicated interfaces.

The expensive universal remote I had purchased to simplify watching television is brilliant, but it has an Achilles heel. It works correctly only if all the devices are turned off. If any of the devices are already on, the remote turns off that device.

If you have a good mental model of how the system works, your conscious brain can diagnose and fix the problem. Unfortunately, when multiple products from multiple vendors must work together, the novice user typically has no idea where to begin when the system doesn't work as expected. In our increasingly complex world, we commonly use a product designed by one company, a software application designed by another, and an accessory designed by yet another company. It is important to provide the user with an intuitive representation of how the products work together and what to do when they don't.

Because unconscious mental processes have always been invisible to conscious evaluation, many products understandably create aggravation for the user. Exacerbating this problem is that fact that engineers design most of the devices with which we must interact. Engineers are not like the rest of us. Their approach to problem solving relies heavily on the executive mind (indeed, this is a key selection criteria for becoming an engineer), and their extensive experience with a product causes them to unconsciously create habitual mastery. What looks natural to the engineer appears impenetrable to the user.

Arguably, the primary culprit in the creation of overly complicated products is the organizational structure of the firm. The executive brain approaches problems logically and systematically, and the executive organizing a company can be counted on to create a logical division of labor that looks good on a chart. But again, the logic of the executive mind is not the way the habitual mind works.

One of my clients is a Fortune 100 company with 60,000 employees. We were attempting to craft a simple experiment to test a new sales concept in a retail environment. The study could have been done in a week with two people to get the information we were looking for. But we fell into the silo-world of this company's organizational structure. Seven months lapsed from the times we met with customer experience, retail strategy, customer contact, and legal, and the time we actually got into the store. During that time, the study morphed beyond recognition.

The organizational structures of most large companies make it difficult to deliver products that work well with the dinosaur brain. The offering is created by multiple organizations broken into functional groups, each filled with smart, well-intentioned, hard-working employees interpreting the product goal differently. When this process involves multiple companies, the likelihood that the outcome will be intuitive is reduced even more.

The costs of this approach extend beyond the customer's experience. Companies must support their overly complicated products, including the costs of training sales and support personnel. Calls into customer service can cost anywhere from $8 to $20, adding to the hidden expense of poor design. A failure to understand and design for the dinosaur brain is a leading cause of frustration for customers and ultimately the failure of so many products, services, and web sites.

The logic of the executive mind is exceptionally powerful in designing systems and solutions. You cannot hope to manage hundreds or thousands of employees without crafting something that resembles an organization chart delineating responsibilities and lines of authority. The problem comes when this defines how you design for and interact with customers.

Simply put, you must design the physical product to work with the habitual mind so that the executive mind is free to focus on the task. This applies to designing web sites and software interfaces as well. Make sure the original vision for the product is maintained by having one manager with the responsibility and authority to give thumbs up or down to each department's contribution.

A Norman Door into the Two Minds of the Customer

Donald Norman has become synonymous with poor design. He continuously receives communications from readers who have discovered a "Norman door" or a "Norman switch," which are devices that challenge the cognitive skills of the user. On his web site (www. jnd.com) and in books and articles, Norman serially chronicles poorly designed products. He can find design flaws in a hotel door in Amsterdam or the layout of a building in London, but his forte is in the world of high technology. To combat what he sees as the creeping complexity of technology-driven products such as the iDrive, Norman has long championed human-centered design.

"There is a difference between complicated and complex," he explained to me in a wide-ranging discussion. "Complexity is not the problem; that's what's on the inside of the box. The problem comes when we make what's on the outside of the box complicated." When I asked him if complicated interfaces were simply a product of complex technology or numerous vendors collaborating on the same device, he bristled. Norman sees the failure to understand and design for the habitual mind as a recurring theme in the information age.

"Overly complicated interfaces are the product of poor design," he insisted, "though they can also occur as a byproduct of organizational structure. Companies have different goals than do their customers. Take cell phones—the handset manufacturers have one set of goals, the wireless service providers a completely different set of goals. And there are other parties involved who create applications, and still others that make accessories. The poor customer is left befuddled." He used a camera phone to make the point.

"When you take a picture with your telephone, the task is pretty clear. You want to save, throw away, or email the picture. You don't want to go through a series of menus to select the right action; you want those choices right there, right in front of you. A task-oriented design would do just that. A logically oriented design would have everything neatly tucked away in menus, unnecessarily complicating your life."

Norman refers to the underlying design philosophies as taxonomic versus "taskonomic." A taxonomic approach creates categories and subcategories that group like things together, while a taskonomic method organizes around the activity. "Taxonomic structures are appropriate outside of contexts—for example, in libraries and hardware stores. But they are ill suited for supporting an activity," Norman explained. "In a hardware store, nails are put with other nails, but when a carpenter is working on the job, the nails are kept next to the hammer."

When I asked him if the taxonomic approach is a byproduct of the company's organizational chart, he agreed: "There is an old saying that the organization of a product reflects the organizational structure of the company."

For Norman, there is no reason to think of taxonomic and taskonomic orientations as mutually exclusive. Companies must understand when to design for the executive mind and when to design for the habitual mind.

For Norman, good design appeals to the multiple minds inside the brain. In his book *Emotional Design,* he identifies this as processing a product on three levels: visceral, behavioral, and reflective. These layers correspond to the dinosaur brain, the limbic system, and the cerebrum.

According to Norman, the visceral layer is reflexive and fast, with virtually no processing involved. The behavioral level can involve highly complex scripts reflecting learned behavior, but it is not conscious. In Norman's view, conscious thought is the exclusive territory of the reflective level but does not directly influence behavior. "The reflective level is the top, conscious self, but it doesn't directly access sensory input. It monitors and influences but does not directly control."

Norman's message to work with the conscious and unconscious minds is directed primarily at designers, but its relevance to marketers, managers, and executives is equally valid. At one point in our discussion, I began a comment with, "If executives accept this premise ..." and he completed the thought with, "they will have to reorganize the company."

The organizational structure of the firm should reflect the optimum approach to the marketplace, with a high priority on serving a well-defined group of customers. If your company's organization is geared to the executive mind, there is a good chance that your products are as well.

The Limbic System: Where Habits Form and Live

Wrapped around the dinosaur brain is a remarkable set of structures collectively known as the limbic system. Sandwiched between the oldest and newest parts of the brain, this region of the brain, more than any other, will determine the reception your product receives in the marketplace. This is where memories are formed and habits are learned. It is also the center of emotional experience.

This section starts by outlining how habits are formed in the basal ganglia. This process underlies the role of habits in customer behavior. By understanding how habits are formed, stored, and activated, managers will understand what they must do to make their products a habit instead of a choice.

Next, we examine how the hippocampus creates, stores, and retrieves memories. We also explore how the amygdala, the center of strong emotions, shapes what we choose to store in memory and what we recall.

Habits and the Basal Ganglia

The power of habits can be seen in the waistlines of Americans: Sixty percent of us are overweight. We spend $50 billion a year on weight loss products, plus additional billions on gym memberships, exercise DVDs, and fitness equipment. And yet less than 10% of Americans who set out to lose weight are successful.

Alarmed by rising health-care costs associated with the national bulge, legislators and regulators crafted an expensive and futile plan to change behavior through information and education. The National Labeling and Education Act was passed in 1990 in the misguided belief that if people knew what was in their food, it would change their behavior. Hundreds of millions of labeling dollars later, we're still getting fatter.

Although experts provide a litany of reasons for our obesity, the primary culprit is a fist-sized bundle of neurons in your brain called the basal ganglia. Most of what we do, including eating and exercise (or a lack thereof), is a product of habits stored in this specific part of the limbic system.

First, let's get a clear idea of exactly what constitutes a habit. Habits can be simple or complex behaviors. They are learned slowly over time through repetition. Once learned, a habit is activated by a cue that is associated with a context-dependent stimulus. The phone rings; you answer it. Someone extends his hand to you; you shake it. When a habit is formed, it can be executed with little or no conscious intervention. A habit might become dormant, but it does not disappear—instead, it hides, like a sleeper agent ready to be reawakened.

The impetus of this book came from a casual observation of watching my teenage daughter use her cell phone while sitting on the couch beside the cordless landline. I watched her initiate the call and realized she wasn't make a judgment about call quality—and, being a teenager, she certainly wasn't thinking about cost. She used her cell phone out of habit. I was doing a presentation a couple weeks later for a group of telecommunications executives and used the idea of becoming your customers' habit instead of their choice as my theme. The highly positive response I received led me to think maybe I was on to something. I thought habits might be a clever idea, fodder for an article or a short book.

But then I encountered the work of Dr. Ann Graybiel and discovered that the study of habits had been elevated to brain science.

Graybiel is the Walter A. Rosenblith Professor of Neuroscience at MIT and is director of the Graybiel Laboratory at the Department of Brain and Cognitive Sciences McGovern Institute for Brain Research. She received the National Medal of Science in 2001, the highest recognition for scientific achievement in the United States. Most significantly (for our purposes), Graybiel is almost single-handedly responsible for unlocking the mysteries of the region of the brain responsible for habits.

For more than three decades, Graybiel has studied the basal ganglia. Although she has availed herself of all the new technologies, her breakthroughs largely came from traditional methods, using mice, mazes, and small electrodes. After considerable trial and error, Graybiel and her associates were able to identify specific neurons in a mouse's basal ganglia that fired when the mouse was learning to navigate a maze.

But the firing patterns of these neurons were puzzling. When the mouse was first put into the maze, the neuron fired constantly, as if everything in the maze might be important. After a few repetitions, the mouse learned to associate a left turn when a tone was sounded. When this task was mastered, the firing patterns of those same neurons changed. Instead of firing throughout the maze, they fired only at the beginning and the end of the task. When the mouse was covering the ground it knew, not only were the basal ganglia neurons quiet, but so were surrounding neurons that normally contributed noise to the system.

How do the firing patterns of neurons inside a mouse's brain change the foundations of marketing? Graybiel's research uncovered the primacy of habits in controlling behavior. She and others have shown that the basal ganglia in our minds work much the same way as they do in these mice. When we repeat a behavior, even one that involves many independent steps, it is etched into the basal ganglia, ready to be activated whenever a cue is encountered. When that learning occurs, we no longer need to consciously attend to it—we are on autopilot.

Graybiel calls this "chunking" behavior, like buckling your seatbelt and backing out the driveway. The marketing challenge here is that we can't see what's going on inside our own basal ganglia. If you were asked to describe getting into your car this morning, you probably wouldn't consciously remember putting on your seatbelt, putting the car in reverse, looking through the rear window, or using your mirrors. The cue-laden contexts of your daily routine activate these chunks of behavior. The cue can be something external in the environment or can arise from an internal state, such as hunger. The placement of impulse purchase items near the checkout counters of many stores demonstrates the power of cues to trigger behavior. If you're hungry, it's hard to resist those candy bars by the cash register.

This habitual system is working underneath your executive mind, responding to cues that the executive mind does not even know about. This is what makes habits so hard to break; they often occur before our conscious mind can intervene.

But what happens if the reward is removed, if the habit is no longer reinforced? For rats that had been trained to turn toward a reward (Belgian chocolate is their favorite) when they heard a tone, removing the reward eventually ended the habitual behavior. Again, the neurons in the basal ganglia fired continuously when a rat went through the maze. However, if the reward was reintroduced, the entire habitual process reemerged automatically. When a habit is etched into the basal ganglia, it might become dormant, but it does not go away.

A particularly clever marketing campaign illustrates how cues can activate long-sleeping behaviors. A few years ago, I was working in my home office when I heard the theme song from *I Dream of Jeannie* coming from the television in another room. Although I had not heard that music for decades, I was drawn at a near run, only to discover a commercial for a hamburger chain. As a child, *I Dream of Jeannie* was a favorite of mine, and its theme music, played at the beginning of each episode, served as a cue to get me to the TV. The creators of that commercial might not have known that they were manipulating the basal ganglia, but they knew what they were doing.

How is it that habits are so persistent? Eric Kandel has the answer. The Viennese-born scientist was on his way to becoming a psychiatrist and psychoanalyst when a simple question sidetracked him: What is the biological foundation of memory? Discovering the answer to that question occupied him for decades and led to his receiving the Nobel Prize for Physiology or Medicine in 2000.

Dr. Kandel chose an even simpler animal to study than Graybiel's mice, the sea snail Aplysia. He bucked the popular thought of the day that we couldn't learn much about the human mind by studying simple animals. The advantage in studying the snail is that it has a few large neurons that are easily observable. Kandel believed that the simplicity of the snail's system would make it possible to understand the role neurons play in memory, and that he would be able to generalize these finding to mammals like us. His bet paid off—the lowly snail provided remarkable insights into how we learn.

What Kandel discovered is critical for managers and marketers to understand: Long-term memories are formed when the connetions between neurons are strengthened. For habits, this process occurs in the basal ganglia. Conscious memories are formed in the nearby hippocampus.

But neurons are not always about excitement; sometimes they are about restraint, inhibiting the likelihood of a message being sent along the neural highway. You can see the impact of this dual system by watching someone drinking too much at a party. Alcohol is a depressant, but it depresses inhibitory neurons before excitatory neurons. This accounts for the normally quiet Jim becoming increasingly loud and boisterous before eventually mellowing out and falling to sleep.

We can ignore most of the stimuli impinging on our nervous system because of two properties of neurons. The first is that the resting state of a neuron is tilted toward not firing. For one neuron to communicate with another neuron, the excitation needs to become stronger than the inhibition. A stimulus has to go above some threshold before a neuron will fire—that is, release a chemical neurotransmitter to stimulate the next neuron. The second component is that neurons learn to ignore an irrelevant stimulus.

Most of the time, when a stimulus gets noticed, a local reaction occurs (as with pulling your hand away from a hot plate), but then the neurons return to their normal state. But Kandel discovered that if the stimulus is particularly intense and repeated, that process is modified. Neurons learn. In our DNA, a process says, "Hey, that's important. I should remember that for the future."

Learning occurs when the neuron goes through a physical change. The DNA within the cell sends a message to strengthen the connection between particular neurons. Of course, we can learn in the opposite way. We might learn that a stimulus is unimportant, strengthening inhibitory neuron pathways. Our urban and suburban lives require us to learn to ignore the vast cacophony of the modern world, from lawn mowers to jet engines.

Why is it important for marketers to understand how this process works? Because the success or failure of all your marketing efforts come down to whether you are making a lasting impression on your customers. This is the mechanism that determines whether your advertising gets remembered, your store gets frequented, or your web site gets navigated. Billions of dollars are wasted annually on advertising and promotion that does nothing but contribute to the background noise.

The brain has specialized functions in the various structures that we have touched on briefly. Graybiel's work demonstrated that habits are learned in the basal ganglia, while other researchers have demonstrated that the hippocampus is essential for creating and storing conscious memories. Other parts of the brain are responsible for storing specific types of memories. For example, although visual memories are stored in the back of the brain, a very specific area at the bottom of the brain seems to specialize in recognizing faces. We explore the importance of this to branding in the upcoming section on memory.

The executive mind can learn relatively quickly, whereas habitual learning is slow. However, when the strengthening of neural circuits in the basal ganglia forms a habit, it is persistent. Other learned responses might be etched into the brain, but the old ones do not simply fade away, as evidenced by the power of a 40-year-old TV theme song to draw me like a moth to a flame-broiled burger.

In working with the habitual mind, marketers must understand this process. Habits are built over time through repetition and reside latent primarily in the region of the brain referred to as the basal ganglia. Habits help us to be more mentally efficient by automating behaviors we have encountered previously.

Most of our behavior is the result of habitual responses to cues in the environment. These habits are formed over time. Marketers must create habits by getting customers to repeat behaviors enough times to create changes in the neural circuits of the brain.

The consequences of the tracks laid down in our habitual minds are visible in our shopping behavior. The next section reveals how a major consumer research company is using habits to help its customers understand their customers.

Researching Nielsen Research

AC Nielsen, part of the Nielsen Company, has been examining consumer behavior since 1923. Like so many market researchers, Nielsen's Alastair Gordon was exasperated by the inability of customers to explain their purchase behavior. His initial response to hearing a customer say, "I don't really know why I bought that," was to torture the data, interrogate subjects like suspects in a major crime, or psychoanalyze them. Eventually, it began to dawn on him that maybe consumers didn't know why they bought a lot of what they bought. Worse, maybe they didn't even care.

"Customers do not waste huge amounts of brainpower to make most everyday decisions," Gordon contends. Customers are familiar with thousands of brands, and it occurred to him that instead of looking at what they bought, maybe he should look at the process of buying. He turned to heuristic theory to see if maybe customers were employing simple rules when they shopped instead of using a brand-centric approach. A heuristic can be thought of as a rule of thumb, a simple and versatile tool used to solve a problem—such as buying well-known brands when on sale.

Out of these insights, Gordon and fellow Nielsen consultant Duncan Stuart developed DeltaQual, a research methodology designed to reveal how consumers make decisions based on rules, with brands serving as just one component of a mental formula. The foundations of DeltaQual analysis are Omega rules and Delta moments.

Omega rules are the heuristics that customers learn over time but often forget, the foundations of their habits. When shoppers are using Omega rules, they are effectively on "autopilot." Occasionally, events in the marketplace challenge Omega rules, a process Nielsen calls Delta moments.

A Delta moment occurs when a habitual pathway is disrupted and conscious evaluation replaces automatic response. During a Delta moment, a customer is open to new choices.

"We start with behavior," Nielsen's Achala Srivatsa explained to me while sitting in her Manhattan office. "We try not to ask, 'Why?'" Asking a customer why they bought something automatically engages their executive mind. As discussed in Chapter 1, customers are generally unaware of the habits that guide them. If given a nudge in the direction of conscious guesswork, customers will be unable to recall the information necessary for Nielsen researchers to understand their Omega rules. "Similarly, respondents in focus groups are going to rationalize their decisions, so we avoid them in the early stages of our analysis," Srivatsa noted.

Accordingly, the DeltaQual process begins by finding out how the behavior fell into place. "We use situation reconstruction, the same technique the police use to interview witnesses," Srivatsa explained to me. Using one-to-one interview techniques, the researcher attempts to get the subject to recall the first use of the product. Emphasis is given to remembering sensory information associated with initial experiences. This information is then used in the next step of the process, in which dual interviewers conduct mini focus groups.

Srivatsa explained that, most of the time, customers are on autopilot as they navigate through a store. But interestingly, she noted that people might have very different rules working to explain the same behavior. "A shopper on autopilot may have a very strong brand preference, what we call brand bonding. Or that same behavior might reflect a consumer who has automated that choice out of sheer indifference, what we call inertia driven."

Similarly, Nielsen identifies segments of customers who are in "experimental mode during shopping." Srivatsa listed motivational segments for Delta moments—bargain, buzz, and variety seeking.

In bargain mode, customers are looking for the best deal. If you have ever gone to the store excited to try out a product you've seen or heard about, you are in buzz mode. The third form of experimental shopping is variety seeking. If you like to try out microbrewed beer or new flavors of ice cream, you are engaging the shopping experience with your executive mind tuned to new sensations. This differs from buzz, which is narrowly focused around the goal of trying a specific product that you've heard about.

These segments are not groups of people, but groups of behavior. A customer might be brand-bonded to her toothpaste, inertia driven for cereal purchases, and a bargain shopper for toiletries, yet be looking forward to trying a new flavor of ice tea.

"By understanding the rules, you understand how to strengthen them or how to break them," Srivatsa said. The rules may be trivial yet deterministic. "We found in one market, the size of the coffee granules was a critical heuristic." Conversely, the heuristic may be quite important. "If a baby product ever causes a rash, a mother will never purchase that brand again."

In my dissertation research, six months spent interviewing customers in two consumer electronics chains, this phenomenon was encountered repeatedly. In returning a car stereo from a well-known manufacturer, one customer explained that when he had taken the unit out of the box, "the buttons felt cheap." The feel of the buttons communicated more powerfully than the well-known brand or premium price.

For market leaders, the goal is to prevent Delta moments. New brands or companies attempting new market entry must create Delta moments if they are to break the habits that guide existing consumer behavior.

Whereas DeltaQual focuses on purchase behavior in all of its variety, a couple social psychologists at Duke have set out to discover just how much of behavior is habitual.

Habits and Goals: Wendy Wood

Wendy Wood, Ph.D., began her academic career studying attitudes, a traditional and well-trodden path for a social psychologist.

Her habit epiphany came when a graduate student colleague at a conference she was attending pointed out an obvious flaw in the study of attitudes. People have strong attitudes about working out and getting healthy, but these attitudes are poor predictors of actual behavior. In talking with Wood, I was struck by how similar her journey to habits was to my own upon discovering that customer satisfaction did a poor job of predicting repurchase.

Sitting in her office in the historic Erwin Square Mill Building, Wood walked me though her path to understanding the centrality of habits to human behavior. "Originally, I looked at habits in their pernicious form: Why is it so difficult to stop doing things that are bad for you? But the more I studied them, the more I realized that habits are not only useful, but essential." In addition, her study of habits helped her understand why attitudes and intentions do such a bad job of predicting actual behavior.

"Habits emerge from the gradual learning of associations between an action and outcome, and the contexts that have been associated with them. Once the habit is formed, various elements from the context can serve as a cue to activate the behavior, independent of intention and absent of a particular goal," she explained. "Very often, the conscious mind never gets engaged."

One school of thought even contends that much of our conscious interpretation of our behavior occurs after it happens, Harvard's Daniel Wegner refers to this as "the illusion of conscious will." Although it's counterintuitive, this explains many of the gaps in market research. Let's look at a hypothetical business challenge to see how habitual behavior can sabotage marketing's best efforts.

Imagine that a fast food restaurant notices that in-store sales are flat or declining. Looking at trends in the marketplace, it is suggested that the aging baby boom population is becoming more health conscious. The company decides to evaluate a new, healthy menu item. First, attitudinal research is done to gauge customer interest. Participants in the study are asked if they would be interested in a low-fat and/or low-carbohydrate alternative on the restaurant's menu. They respond favorably to the idea. A low-fat/low-carb sandwich is developed and tests well with focus groups. The project is green-lighted.

After a multimillion-dollar launch that includes heavy advertising and promotion, the sales of the healthy sandwich are dismal. A post-mortem is held to evaluate customer feedback and determine what went wrong, but little is gleaned from the data. Eventually, everyone shrugs and wonders how such a slam-dunk idea ended up wasting millions of dollars.

What happened? When answering the interviewer's question, the respondent answered truthfully from the executive mind's perspective, which knows healthy food is better for her and that her favorite jeans don't fit anymore. "Yes, I would definitely eat the healthy sandwich, if it were available." But here we can see why intentions are not highly correlated to actual behavior.

Fast food restaurants contain hundreds of cues tapping into habitual behavior, like the smell of French fries and high-fat burgers. Before the conscious mind becomes engaged, the customer orders her usual combo meal and, because of another external cue, unthinkingly says, "Yes" when asked if she would like it supersized. If this customer had planned on eating "healthy" today, she may even feel guilt and shame over her behavior and chastise herself for being weak. This is the executive mind assuming that it is in control and taking the blame for the habitual mind's actions.

"Habits become associated with cues in the environment, and so, to some extent, they become separated from goals," Wood explained to me. Although in this example habits seem to be compelling us negatively, we can think through the benefits of this system.

Imagine that a dad takes his three kids to a fast food restaurant for lunch on a Saturday. The place is jammed with kids; the background noise is deafening, and each of his children is talking at the same time. Upon reaching the counter with a mass of humanity at his back hoping he won't have any special orders, he looks at the billboard-sized menu that spans the entire wall. Instead of the executive mind being overwhelmed by the surrounding chaos and the number of choices, the habitual mind takes charge and orders three kid's meals and one adult combo meal. Any attempt to engage his executive mind would hold up the system and prolong the chaos.

Wood has conducted numerous studies with a wide variety of subjects to find out just how much of our daily behavior is under the influence of habits. Participants are provided with pagers and a notebook. Once an hour throughout the day for a week or more, participants are paged. Their assignment is to write down where they are, what they are doing, and what they are thinking. The results are illuminating.

"Whether we're talking about college students or people in the community, 45% of the behaviors participants listed in their diaries tended to be repeated in the same location almost every day," Wood told me. "We can see this is habitual behavior, as participants report thinking about something other than what they are doing." She finds that a quote from D. J. Townsend and T. G. Bever nicely sums up this line of research: "Most of the time what we do is what we do most of the time."[6]

David Neal, Wood's colleague and frequent co-author on habits, joined us for lunch. Neal is a young Australian post-doctorate who met Wood at a conference in Sydney in 2003. She persuaded him to study habits and lured him to Duke, where he now runs the Social Science Research lab. He and Wood are looking into how the brain resolves conflicts between habits and goals.

"We think that people have two behavioral control systems—a habit system and a goal system—that compete for control of behavior," Neal explained. "If you raise motivations, you can interfere with highly routinized behavior. The classic example comes in sports,

---

[6] D. J. Townsend and T. G. Bever, *Sentence Comprehension: The Integration of Habits and Rules* (Cambridge: MIT Press, 2001).

where an athlete chokes, as when a golfer misses an easy 3-foot put to lose a championship."

The relationship between habits and goals occupies much of Wood's thinking. "Habits and goals often work together, as you would expect. But they also work in opposition. When they do, it is typically the strength of the habit that determines which wins." If habits are weak, a person's goals will have a good chance of driving behavior. But if habits are moderate to strong, they typically express themselves even if the behavior is in opposition to a person's morals and beliefs.

Wood is also working with Mindy Ji at Iowa State on understanding how the competing systems vie for behavioral control in consumer purchasing situations. They have found that when a strong habit becomes established, such as when a customer has repeatedly purchased a product in the same context, intentions no longer predict purchase. "A consumer's favorable or unfavorable intention with respect to the product purchase exerted no influence on the consumer's behavior. Of course, people will still express a clear intention, if asked." This is similar to Nielsen's findings that show that the probability of purchasing a product in the future goes up significantly based on the number of times that purchase has been made previously. This repurchase behavior does not correlate strongly to customer satisfaction or intention.

Wood and Ji's results explain why market research has not done a good job of predicting actual consumer behavior. When we ask questions of our customers, we access only one of the two systems vying for control of purchase behavior, and it is often the weaker of the two. Intentions and preferences are not unimportant, but when a strong habit has been established, a cue activates the behavior before the executive mind can exert control.

To better understand how such systems compete within the brain, we next look at our different memory systems and how we learn.

Peeking into Human Memory

Our memories seem simultaneously tangible and ephemeral. They define us, yet, under close examination, are surprisingly insubstantial. Companies spend billions to advertise their messages to potential and existing customers, relying on them to remember brands, slogans, claims, prices, and where to buy their products. But our memories are remarkably unreliable; as a result, much of our advertising money is wasted.

Russell Poldrack, Ph.D., is a cognitive neuroscientist at UCLA studying the brain's systems for learning, memory, decision making, and executive functions. A prodigious researcher, Poldrack was awarded the American Psychological Association Distinguished Scientific Award for Early Career Contributions within a decade of completing his doctorate at the University of Illinois. Poldrack uses the tools of cognitive neuroscience, including fMRI, to tease out what is going on inside our brains as we think, learn, reason, and remember. I talked with Poldrack about the state of current research on memory and learning, and just what exactly we can know from fMRI studies.

"The early evidence for multiple memory systems came from amnesia patients who could not recall information previously presented, but could often perform normally on indirect tests of memory," Poldrack explained. "The existence of multiple memory systems is now firmly established. The current thinking is that we have conscious memories for facts and events supported by a declarative memory system that relies upon the hippocampus and other medial temporal lobe structures. We also have unconscious learning that is supported by nondeclarative or procedural memory mechanisms that rely on widespread cortical and subcortical structures."

Explicit memories are broken into semantic memories of facts and episodic memories of the events in our lives. Implicit memories include skills and habits, classic stimulus-response conditioning, and a fascinating process called priming, in which the brain seems to preload information based on hints picked up from the environment, in what some researchers call remembering the future.

Of particular interest to marketers and managers is that researchers have discovered that structures previously associated with the habitual mind play a significant role in how explicit memories are processed, stored, and retrieved.

Can technology read our minds?

The proliferation of articles with titles like, "This is your Brain on Politics," and "This is your Brain on Brands," gives the false impression that we can use neuroimaging technologies to read minds. I discussed what is knowable using functional magnetic resonance imagining with one of its most notable practitioners, UCLA's Russell Poldrack.

"Functional magnetic resonance imaging doesn't show us individual neurons firing," Poldrack explained. "Instead, we see increased blood flow to those regions of the brain that are activated. Unfortunately, while the mental processes we're interested in occur within a few hundred milliseconds, it takes seconds before the fMRIs can create an image. So what we are seeing in these images might simply be the aftermath of the cognitive processes we are trying to see."

Because of this, researchers rely on a process of reverse-inference, where they work backwards to deduce what brain regions are involved with different types of tasks. While this methodology helps researchers formulate better hypotheses, it doesn't 'prove' that a specific region of the brain performs a specific mental task. But journalists, and more than a few researchers, often report their findings as if inference was truth.

"Though reverse-inference can provide useful information, it is not a logically valid form of deductive reasoning," Poldrack explained. "We are making guesses and hypotheses. We may think we know, but it's not the truth."

I asked him if it might be possible to read minds in the future. "It depends on what you mean by reading minds. We can with fairly good accuracy tell what kind of mental task you are performing, say reading words versus making decisions about

money. However, we are very far away from being able to identify specific thoughts. I hate to say never, but someone will have
to come up with new imaging technology. We're talking at least
decades."

Poldrack encourages researchers to adopt a rigorous statistical
methodology and stresses the importance of the peer review
process to validate work done in this complicated area.

An example of the type of overstatement that worries Poldrack
can be found in a *New York Times* Op-ed piece that appeared
early in the 2008 presidential election cycle. A group of researchers claimed that a study they conducted with 20 subjects
placed in an MRI machine revealed important insights in how
voters viewed the candidates. Poldrack and a group of neuroscientists wrote a letter in response pointing out that the authors
overstated the science. Tellingly, the original article stated that
their research indicated that Mitt Romney shows great potential to win over voters, while Barack Obama and John McCain
elicited very little reaction.

How the Executive Mind Remembers

If you were asked to name the capital of France, this would tap
into your semantic memory. Remembering the trip you took to Paris
accesses your episodic memory. But which type of memory is more influential in deciding what to buy? Before we can answer that question,
we need to understand what makes us remember.

What is a memory? It is not a piece of information stored verba-
tim in your brain like data on a hard drive to be recalled whenever
needed. Just as habits are formed by changes in the synaptic strength
between neurons, memories involve a strengthening of connections
between the specialized cells of the brain, as if our experiences are
etched in our minds. Memories can vary in strength and accuracy, and
they are susceptible to decay and error. Memories are not so much retrieved as they are re-created; they change each time they are brought
into conscious awareness, as in an internal game of Rumor.

While I was a hospital administrator in San Antonio, I benefited regularly from the imprecision of memory. Whenever my competitor hospitals ran advertising, most notably television commercials, our phone rang. Potential patients were quite sure that it was my hospital that ran the ads, a notion we did not attempt to correct.

How many times have you seen a great commercial, whether for a car, a beer, a phone company, or a pair of shoes, but been unable to remember who made the ad? This is a pervasive phenomenon with advertising, yet it is only one of the great challenges facing businesses that want to communicate with the marketplace.

Nowhere is the distinction between conscious and unconscious mental processes fuzzier than in our understanding of memory. Recent research has revealed the surprising magnitude of the role of emotion in executive-mind function, especially in how we select, encode, and retrieve information.

In the great world of diametrically opposed forces—yin and yang, north and south, male and female, Yankees and Red Sox fans—most would include emotion and reason. Emotion is hot, while reason is cold. Emotional decisions are viewed as poor and brash, while a reasoned decision is superior, or at least defensible. Counterintuitively, Elizabeth Phelps, Ph.D., of New York University shows that emotion is central to cognition, decision making, and memory.[7]

Phelps summarizes the surprising insights gained from cognitive neuroscience that reveals how structures long associated with emotion are integral to all that we think of as executive (rational) mind functions. According to Phelps, emotions tell us what is important to remember, help us recall memories, and are essential to decision making.

---

[7]   Elizabeth A. Phelps, "Emotion and Cognition: Insights from Studies of the Human Amygdala," *Annual Review of Psychology*, 57 (2006): 27–53.

Attention

As discussed earlier, memories are changes etched into our neural pathways. For the executive mind to store a memory, it must first focus attention on what is to be remembered. Attention is to explicit memory what repetition is to implicit memory. Attention is the mechanism we use to select what is important.

Yet how do we decide what stimuli to ignore and what to focus on? What apparatus alerts us to attend to a particular stimulus out of the thousands that bombard our senses at any particular moment? In large part, our emotions tell us what is worthy of attention.

If you were walking down your street and a dog jumped out at you, barking aggressively, it would capture your complete attention. Fear does a great job of concentrating the mind, thereby increasing the likelihood of survival. Other emotions play a similar role. Feelings of disgust keep us away from things that might be harmful. Empathetic feelings such as sadness, joy, love, and sorrow help bind us together, creating a societal culture far stronger than most would-be predators.

Our emotions help us pick out important aspects of the environment, whether they are threats or opportunities. Scanning a crowded party, we automatically pick out a familiar face without conscious effort. Similarly, in that same room, you can hear your name mentioned in a conversation from across the room. Emotion focuses our attention like a lens, prioritizing around threats, but is always open to opportunity.

The world we live in bears little resemblance to the world that shaped our evolution, but a marketer's success depends on appealing to the same attention mechanisms that allowed our ancestors to pick up warning signals from the bush. This means creating associations between specific stimulation of our senses and our emotions' threshold of indifference

Marketing's early successes came from just these types of associations. Brands, logos, and jingles captured shoppers' attention with emotion. By the turn of the twentieth century, several iconic brands had already been established, including P&G and Coke, and marketing as a discipline was born.

However, marketing's success planted the seeds of its own destruction. Companies now pay for 4,500 messages per person per day in the United States, roughly one ad for every 14 seconds you are awake. Thousands of new products are released into grocery stores and department stores each year. Add to this an exponential growth in the number of information outlets and advertising media, and it is easy to see that customers are overwhelmed by the noise. Launching a new product nationally costs tens of millions of dollars. Of course, the more that a company spends, the more noise is added to the system and the more you must spend to rise above the noise. These aren't called vicious cycles for nothing.

The original cognitive psychological meaning of habituation was the lack of response to a stimulus that originally caused a reaction. If you put a mouse in a cage with a stuffed owl, its initial response is great agitation. However, after repeated exposures, the mouse ignores the fake bird. If a brand fails to elicit an emotional response, it will fail to get attention. If you simply ratchet up the noise, the customer becomes accustomed to the increased volume and forms a new threshold of indifference that must be overcome.

To successfully cut through the noise, don't be noise. Understand the emotional component of the brand to your customers, to attract their attention. Keep that emotional connection updated, to prevent your brand from becoming a stuffed owl.

Consolidating Memories

What separates memories that disappear within minutes, days, or weeks from those that last a lifetime? Again, emotion plays a critical role in consolidating memories from short to long term. Emotion prioritizes what is remembered, indexed by the type and intensity of that emotion. Most of us remember the details of our first kiss or where we were that fateful day the Twin Towers were destroyed. But we probably do not remember our 15th kiss or where we were on February 26, 1993, when a 1,500-pound bomb went off in a parking garage of the North Tower. The intensity of our emotional response marks the importance of an event. The more richly an event is categorized by emotion, the longer and more detailed it will be remembered.

Our assumptions of how we learn are shaped largely by our years spent in school. Sitting at a desk five hours a day, 180 days a year for 12 years, plus college and maybe even graduate school, powerfully persuades us that learning involves books, reading, and taking notes. We intentionally store facts and learn rules to solve written problems so we can do well on a test so that we can get a good job, buy a house and a nice car, and take cool trips. Undoubtedly, this helps us survive in the modern world, but this experience convinces us of something that is basically not true: We require language and writing to think and to learn.

Written language has existed for only 5,000 years. Widespread literacy did not emerge until after Gutenberg's printing press in 1455. Studies show that only 15% of the general population cites reading as a preferred method of knowledge acquisition. Yet we bombard our customers with words in ads, flyers, and mailers, and on our web sites.

We think not in words, but in images. We attempt to translate our mental states into language the way a painter attempts to convey a scene with paint, brush, and canvas. No matter how talented the artist is, the painting is as pale a reflection of reality as our words are a pale reflection of our thoughts.

Another problem with communicating with words is that languages have an inherent ambiguity that is exacerbated by our individual and cultural experiences. Traveling through Southeast China, I was surprised when my interpreter, who was native Chinese, could not understand a conversation between two men from another province, even though they were speaking the common language, Mandarin (Putonghua). She explained to me that the language is highly context driven and that, without a shared background, she couldn't really follow what they were saying. They spoke the same words but not the same language.

Not only is thought largely nonverbal, but so are most communications. Experts contend that as much as 80% of communication is nonverbal. We rely on body language, facial expressions, tone, and other clues in the environment to derive meaning. A new type of cell discovered in the 1990s appears to explain the neurological bases of this nonverbal exchange of information.

Mirror neurons were discovered accidentally in a research laboratory in Parma, Italy, by researchers monitoring motor neurons in monkeys. The researchers had isolated a particular neuron that fired whenever a monkey reached for a peanut, an experiment they had run numerous times. But then something very surprising happened. In view of the monkey, a hungry researcher reached for a peanut, and that isolated neuron in the monkey's skull fired exactly as if the monkey were reaching for the peanut. To that particular neuron, the experience of reaching for the peanut was the same as someone else reaching for the peanut.

Upon discovering the same class of cells in humans, a new understanding of our social nature unfolded. If you have ever winced at someone else's discomfort or flinched at a particularly hard hit while watching a football game, you've experienced mirror neurons connecting you to your fellow humans. Mirror neurons provide a direct connection among us, creating a level of intimacy that words can never capture.

The ability of an actor to get us to become emotionally involved in a story is largely a part of this neural empathy built into our brains. It is an entirely unconscious process that profoundly influences our behavior. Director Mel Gibson made *The Passion of the Christ* in a language foreign to the audience—in fact, a language unspoken for a thousand years. Yet James Caviezel's portrayal of Jesus being beaten and humiliated was so powerful that audiences recoiled with each lash of the whip. Part of what makes us human is this powerful connection to others that makes us literally experience their feelings.

How, then, should you communicate with your customers? How do you get customers, who are overwhelmed with sensory input, to remember your web site or where to find you in the department store? Multiple methods exist, and they vary in terms of cost and effectiveness. We expand on this topic in Chapter 6, "Habit and Marketing Management," but it is worth touching upon these ideas while these concepts are fresh.

The brute-force way to remember something is through repetition. If you repeat any message enough times, it will be remembered. Irritating but effective commercials such as "Ring Around the Collar" and "Head On" get us to remember their slogan by endless repetitions. We can also encase our message in easily remembered packages such as rhymes, alliteration, and jingles. The two primary limitations of this approach are expense and complexity. Repeating a message enough times for a disinterested audience to remember it is prohibitively expensive for all but the most widely used brands. The other problem with repetition is that the message cannot be very complex. The longer the message, the more repetitions are required for it to become etched into memory. This is why experts recommend limiting slogans to three words (Just Do It)—four at the most (Soup Is Good Food).

Alternatively, we can communicate more effectively through the use of story, metaphor, and emotion. Although advertisers have long understood this, their messages are often painted on rather than baked in. Flip through any magazine, and you will encounter an emotion-filled picture that has little to say about the product being advertised. Advertisers know that emotionally powerful images such as a baby, attractive face or a puppy will get your attention, but the message must somehow relate to the image if the ad is to work. Michelin's ad campaign showing babies riding in tires grabs attention, but the slogan drives the point: "Because so much is riding on your tires." The emotional content is carried over from the ad to the product.

Storing memories is a process. The more richly the information is contextualized, the more it will be remembered. Create a process that connects the brand meaningfully to an emotion in your communications. Evaluate your reliance on text, even to your business customers.

But after it's stored, how do we get our customers to recall the information when we need them to?

Retrieving Memories

Not only does emotion get us to pay attention and let us know what to remember, but it also facilitates recall. In numerous research studies, emotionally charged images, words, and stories are remembered better and longer than their neutral counterparts. The link between memory and emotion appears to be a two-way street. Just as recalling strong emotions can facilitate memory of events, memory of events can cue those same emotions.

The great challenge is linking the retrieval of specific memories at critical times during purchase and consumption (or utilization). To put this into Nielsen's DeltQual framework, how do we get customers to remember the persuasive part of our communications during a Delta moment when they are not shopping on autopilot?

We must avoid the mental model that a customer makes a rational comparison of product attributes, as if making a list of pros and cons. Most decisions happen very rapidly, with significant processing done outside conscious awareness. My editor told me of research that suggests that a book has three seconds to grab a reader's attention in the store, and that book buyers for the major chains give a book only 20 seconds of attention before deciding whether to buy. So much for not judging a book by its cover.

These quick decisions are not bad decisions; they are simply a strategy for survival in a world cluttered with decisions (just look at the number of coffee choices at Starbucks). To make sure customers tap into the decision rules that include considering your product, make sure you understand their decision rules. You must then communicate that your product fulfills that rule, preferably with an emotional tag. Then reinforce that message via the distribution channel, whether that is in a store, from a salesperson, or on the Web.

Managers and marketers who try to convince potential customers of their product's superiority by listing product attributes will be as successful as a geeky suitor asking out a cheerleader by including his resumé, SAT scores, and the net present value of his future earnings potential. Remember, your customer is looking for shortcuts to good decisions.

Our ability to store and retrieve conscious memories is also a function of mood, another unconscious state that colors our perception. We store more memories when we are in a good mood than in bad one. Ads close to upbeat stories have a better chance of being remembered than ones that follow tragic news.

Our current mood also impacts what we remember. We recall memories better when our mood at retrieval matches our mood at storage.

Why are our memories so wrapped up in our emotions? The relationship between emotion and memory is easy to understand by looking at the limbic region. The seahorse (hippocampus) is responsible for consolidating episodic memories, while the almond (amygdala) is the center for strong emotion. However, these are not distinct structures. The amygdala is a small bulb that hangs off the end of the hippocampus. Their co-location would suggest that their functions would be interrelated, and fMRI studies reveal this to be so. Only because we assumed for so long that emotion and reason were separate have we failed to integrate them as well as we might in our approach to the marketplace.

Managers and marketers need to understand the intimate relationship between memory, emotion, and decision-making. Customers are trying to create shortcuts to simplify their lives. Do not add to their burden, and do not judge them. Make it easy for them to choose your product and then keep using it without having to think about it.

3 ——————————————————

The PFC: Home to the Executive Mind

The major goal of this book is to shine a light on the hidden influence of the habitual mind in customer behavior. However, the executive mind plays a critical role in most decision making, and marketers must understand how to work with both systems. Because the executive mind can think about only one thing at a time, it hands off routine decisions to the habitual mind. When the habitual mind encounters novelty, it engages the problem-solving abilities of the executive mind. When the executive mind becomes involved, it might take over the entire decision or make a small modification and then return control to the habitual mind.

Wendy Wood's research shows that when habits are strongly formed, they control behavior more predictably than our intentions and goals. If you're a betting person, bet on habits. But the executive mind is still quite powerful, and marketers and managers must understand its influence in all phases of product selection, product use, and product switching.

The cerebrum is the newest and, by far, the largest part of the human brain, fitting like a helmet over the limbic system and not quite encasing the brain stem. Although all the areas of the cerebrum are involved in processing information that is critical to successful marketing, our focus is restricted to the prefrontal cortex (PFC), the region of the brain just above your eyes. The PFC is the home of executive functions, including perception, problem solving, and imagination. It's where the idea of "you" lives.

It's difficult to resist using computer metaphors when discussing the brain because both are information-processing machines. A relatively new development in the World Wide Web provides a metaphor to describe the PFC: the mashup. A mashup is a Web application that combines data from other applications (actually, from application programming interfaces, or APIs) to create a unique representation of information. An early mashup combined Google Map's API with crime statistics by zip code. Enter a zip code, and the mashup displays a map showing where crimes occurred.

The PFC works in much the same way, calling up and combining the vast repositories of information stored throughout the brain. This amazing capability provides the building blocks of language, art, culture, and civilization. It is also the source of our individuality: Even identical twins raised together will mash up their experiences and knowledge to create a unique sense of the world and of self.

Two mechanisms within the PFC strongly influence how information is mashed up: categorization and working memory. Discoveries in how we categorize and the role of working memory promise to radically alter our perceptions of branding, positioning, and advertising.

Imagine that you are planning a special evening with your significant other. Your internal representation of the nature of your relationship and the nature of the evening shape whether you choose to make an intimate dinner at home or make reservations at a restaurant. If you choose to go out, your goal will be to match the restaurant to these internal states—your date mashup.

You can approach this as a categorization-matching problem. The challenge is that restaurants can be categorized in a nearly infinite number of ways: by food type, cost, nationality, geography, past history, reputation, recommendation, ambience, and any combination of attributes. But how do we assign a specific restaurant to a particular category? Why is one restaurant reserved for special events and another chosen for a romantic evening?

As with customer satisfaction surveys and focus groups, asking the question gets you thinking about the answer, which obscures how the process naturally occurs. A specific kind of neuron in the PFC actually accomplishes the process of categorization.

From an evolutionary perspective, it is clearly advantageous for an animal to rapidly categorize another animal as a threat or a meal. Researchers at Massachusetts Institute of Technology (MIT) were able to demonstrate how this process occurs. They showed that individual neurons in the PFC of a monkey's brain tune to specific categories. Monkeys were trained to recognize the generic concept of a cat (a house cat, a cheetah, and a tiger) and a dog (a German Shepard, a Pointer, and a St. Bernard) on a computer monitor. After training, one set of neurons fired when the monkey was presented with images of a cat, and another set of neurons fired when the monkey saw a dog on the monitor. This part of the experiment demonstrates what is referred to as the cell's plasticity—its ability to learn.

Researchers then wrote a program that presented a morphed image that combined various percentages of cat and dog features. When the image was more than 50% dog, the dog category neurons fired. But when the image shifted to more than 50% cat, the dog category neurons were silent and the cat neurons fired. Other areas of the brain were monitoring the physical attributes of these chimeras, but the category neurons were all or nothing.

The categorization process is robust and flexible. On one hand, an object is either in or out of a category, but on the other hand, the category can evolve. We might learn to categorize birds as flying creatures, but we can accommodate penguins and ostriches. We can even create seemingly contradictory categories, such as sugar-free candy and low-fat ice cream. Let's take a look at how category neurons impact our marketing efforts.

Several years ago, a maker of frozen dinners wanted to expand into the frozen desert market, launching a new ice cream with its familiar brand. The business case looked persuasive: The company already had the distribution channels (including refrigerated trucks), longstanding relationships with retailers, and millions of existing customers. They only needed to move a couple of freezer units over in the grocery store. Unfortunately for this company, the real distance they needed to move was not in the store, but in the executive mind.

This company had successfully created a strong but specific brand position with customers—its brand was narrowly described around the concept of frozen dinners. When customers saw the company's brand, they thought mashed potatoes and gravy, not chocolate ripple. The company's hopes for increased profits melted.

How unfair it seems that Healthy Choice is able to move effortlessly all over the grocery. Not only is it in the frozen dinner and ice cream freezers, but it's also in the cookie, soup, and cracker aisles. Healthy Choice created a broad category in the working memory of the executive brain around the idea of healthful food. Its success comes from creating a convenient shortcut for weight-conscious customers.

Understanding how customer segments create categories is essential for branding and positioning. The cell phone was launched in 1983, creating a new product category. One estimate by a prestigious research company predicted that the total market for cell phones by the year 2000 would be only 900,000. The researcher's mistake was to categorize the cell phone as simply another phone. The actual number of cell phones in the United States at the end of 1999 was almost 100 million.

When Apple introduced the Newton in 1993, the very clever device primarily struggled because it didn't lend itself to easy categorization. Several other manufacturers came out with electronic organizers, but not until the Palm Pilot emerged did the category of personal digital assistant (PDA) catch on in a meaningful way. The Newton was brilliant, but it was so far ahead of its time that it was not around when the PDA category became firmly but briefly established.

The PDA did not die as much as it morphed into a new category. When Palm, RIM, and others combined the functionality of PDAs with cell phone capabilities, another new category emerged: the smartphone. When that category was established in the executive minds of business customers, Motorola, Samsung, HTC, and others could gain instant traction by calling their new devices smartphones as well.

Success in creating new categories is elusive, especially for technology companies. Intel and Microsoft have spent millions promoting tablet computers and Ultra Mobile PCs (UMPCs), but neither idea has caught on. Similarly, e-books, Internet appliances, and pen computing have struggled for acceptance. Anybody remember the clear rage of the 1990s that brought us see-through Crystal Pepsi and Miller Clear?

How your product is categorized is critical to your success, but it is only partially under your control. By understanding the rules that customers use to make their category judgments, a company can position its brand appropriately. Most companies attempting to create a category fail. For every Apple iPhone, a hundred Audreys (3Com's short-lived Internet appliance) have failed.

How often do you return to a cookbook while following a recipe? Your answer reflects how well your working memory functions. Working memory enables us to hold on to information long enough to decide what to do with it. If you have ever tried to remember a phone number just long enough to dial it, you know the utility and frustration of working memory. Researchers used to think of this cognitive function as simply short-term memory, a stepping-stone to long-term storage. It is now believed that working memory is a separate function that not only holds on to ideas, but also actively manipulates them in the PFC to solve problems.

As we communicate with customers, whether trying to sell something or explain how a product operates, we are making demands on their working memories. Patricia Goldman-Rakic pioneered our understanding of working memory and its location in the PFC. She called this area the blackboard of the mind, and she described the process as holding certain data "online" so that the working memory can retrieve and manipulate information from other areas of the brain to form new associations at subsequent steps to solve problems. Goldman-Rakic was a brilliant researcher with a tenacious spirit, and her contributions were recognized across the disciplines of psychology, psychiatry, and neuroscience. Tragically, she was killed at 66 while absentmindedly crossing a busy street near her home in Connecticut, her attention undoubtedly on her research.

Many of our marketing efforts fail or succeed as they come to fruition in the working memory of the PFC. Can a potential customer retrieve your brand from memory to consider your company as a solution to the problem she is currently facing? Does your online ordering system overly tax customers' working memory, causing them to abandon their carts before check out? Virtually all our product, promotion, and distribution choices impact our customers' ability to process our offer in their working memories.

Working memory varies significantly among individuals, which is another area where very bright people can make critical mistakes by assuming that their customers think like they do. It's better to assume that your customers would prefer to minimize the need to consciously attend to your products and service. Countless companies have installed automated voice-response systems at the front end of calls into customer service. If you offer more than three or four choices, you have already exceeded the comfort level of most customers' working memory.

Working memory is a finite resource that customers use to compare your company's offer with their needs. The more complicated your message or the more abstract your promise, the more you tax your customers' working memory.

For executives, managers, and marketers, the brain's dual nature goes a long way to explaining many of our most persistent challenges.

We might like to think that the implications of these new insights can be easily transferred into our existing business models, but, unfortunately, that is not the case. We have built our corporations on a flawed understanding of customer behavior. It isn't enough to put up posters saying, "Be the Customer's Habit" and "Beware: Use of Our Product May Be Habit Forming."

Part II

Habits: The New Science of Marketing

4

Of iPods, Habits, and Market Revolution

The marketing theories that guide and influence many of our core business processes are based on an incorrect understanding of how people make consumption decisions.

How the iPod Killed the CD

As with most great successes, in retrospect, the iPod seems inevitable. Between 2001 and 2007, Apple sold more than 110 million of the portable audio dynamos. Its introduction of the iTunes music store in 2003 created another revolution, becoming the number-one web site for legally downloaded music. In a four-year stretch, customers downloaded more than three billion songs through iTunes, along with 100 million TV shows. And its first foray into the cell phone market was such a huge success that the entire handset industry felt the need to respond.

In hindsight, market success is tracked by sales and revenue, easily charted and graphed. But when it comes to predicting future success, any major market shift represents changes in people's habits—that is, in behavior that is controlled by invisible forces. It happens slowly as new habits are formed, often replacing old habits. Developing a product that will create or change people's habits is inordinately difficult. By deconstructing the iPod's growth, we can see how the capability to change habits, not product superiority or pricing, creates the foundation of success.

The success of the iPod was not inevitable. The $100 million in total revenue that the digital audio player market generated in 2000 was a rounding error to the multibillion-dollar music industry. The niche category was born with the development of the MP3 standard, which facilitated the compression of audio files that could then be played on computers. The first MP3 players to catch on, such as Diamond Multimedia's Rio, used flash memory that enabled users to carry the equivalent of one CD on their tiny solid state drives. Young techies had a limited but enthusiastic response to these new devices. MP3 players had the advantage over CD players of not skipping when jostled, making them ideal for running. This segment was already mixing and burning their own playlists to CDs, so it was easy to transfer that behavior to the new devices.

Shortly after the creation of flash-based players, Compaq Computer released the first hard drive–based MP3 player, which was dubbed a Personal Jukebox because it could carry up to 1,200 songs. The market for this device continued to be small but was growing as more people began to transfer their music from individual CDs to their computers and portable devices.

When Apple launched the iPod, the market was not only nascent—it was hostile. Users needed to own a computer and be comfortable with nonintuitive software to "rip" songs from CDs and then transfer them. The music industry viewed the entire product category as a threat and aggressively lobbied against it on the grounds of copyright infringement. Apple's device was more expensive and had less storage than its primary competitors. This makes Apple's success all the more impressive, a success best understood by looking at how its design worked with the habitual mind.

From our new understanding of how the habitual mind works, we can see how critical early decisions laid the foundations for the iPod's eventual domination of the portable music space. The genius of the iPod's design is that it facilitated quick habitual mastery. A complex interface could easily bog down a pocket-size device that held a thousand songs. The iPod's clickwheel was an ingenious solution to both searching for music and controlling volume. Subsequent iPods even integrated the traditional play, pause, and skip buttons into the clickwheel. With just a little practice and no instruction, users could quickly master the device with one hand. Had the device not been so intuitive, users would not have seen the benefit of putting their music libraries on subsequent generation of iPods that would carry not just a thousand songs, but 10,000 or even 40,000, as well as audio books, photos, videos, and podcasts.

Even beyond the iPod design, the iTunes software was also essential to making the iPod such a huge hit. Before iTunes, managing digital music ripped from CDs was the domain of computer-savvy kids. With iTunes, even Luddites could rip, mix, and burn—the company's ad campaign encouraged customers to transfer CDs to their computers so they could make their own playlists. Instead of listening to the music the way record labels decided they should, users could combine their music however they pleased. This built on and then radically expanded the practice of making mix tapes, a slow and awkward analog process.

Slowly, iTunes irrevocably changed the way we listened to music. By fall 2007, more than 600 million copies had been downloaded. The music industry finally came around to seeing the positive side of digitally distributing music. Steve Jobs, Apple's charismatic CEO, cut deals with the major labels that were actively suing other companies trying to digitally distribute their songs. Jobs boasts that iTunes became the third-largest music store in the United States in 2007 and the number-one electronic distributor of music in the 22 countries where the iTunes store operates.

The integration of iTunes with the iPod caused a seismic shift inside our brains. Records, eight-tracks, tapes, and CDs had conditioned us to think in an album format—a music serving size of 10 to

12 songs. Now our life could have its own soundtrack. And when our personal soundtrack was on a device that could fit into our pocket, the idea of a CD became quaint. We soon chose to forego radio, connecting iPods to stereos and turning us all into amateur DJs. Major automobile manufacturers have even modified their vehicles to accept iPods, and Nike specifically developed a running shoe to output running statistics to the iPod platform of devices.

The power of habits is that they guide our behavior, influencing what we do without conscious awareness. Virtually all marketplace success comes from creating a product or service that customers use habitually. What sets Apple apart in its foray into portable music is that it created an ecosystem that controls habits. By tying iTunes to multiple generations of iPods and the iPhone, Apple has created the rarest of successes in a hypercompetitive marketplace, a sustainable competitive advantage.

The iPod has been repeatedly slammed for numerous shortcomings. Its audio encoding system has been derided for poor quality, its price as insupportable compared to alternatives, and the entire business model as a bad deal for customers. Such attacks are common because experts are evaluating products with their executive minds, without understanding that habits are not created based on weighing a list of pros and cons. Analysts, pundits, and industry experts generally argue against reality. According to the truly knowledgeable, the clearly superior product always seems to lose out to some deeply flawed offering that has somehow managed to fool the public.

This section of the book updates foundational marketing principles based on our current understanding of how the executive and habitual minds work in tandem through every facet of customer behavior.

5

Marketing from a Habitual Perspective

So far I've been picking on marketing, which is really not my intent. I believe that marketing is the soul of the company, the link between an organization and the customers it serves. Our marketing leadership produced much of the United States' global success. The advent of marketing in the early twentieth century is inexorably tied to that era's growth and burgeoning prosperity.

Yet when we look at the current standard of marketing productivity, the discipline clearly needs a jump-start. Chapter 1, "How Habits Undermine Marketing," listed a few of marketing's problems, such as high new product failure rate, vast sums of wasted advertising dollars, and an inability to hold on to customers in spite of delivering a highly satisfying experience. Unfortunately, this is considered acceptable— it's the cost of doing business. However, by applying the knowledge from brain sciences covered previously, we can radically improve marketing's performance.

The Failure of Customer Satisfaction

Academics, consultants, and authors often make bold statements to grab attention. The following statement is simply a well-documented fact:

Customer satisfaction is essentially meaningless and a waste of time to measure, pursue, and achieve.

In the course of human activity, an intuitively appealing but unproven idea can become so well accepted that it drives behavior without critical analysis. At their heart, radical breakthroughs penetrate such assumptions. The belief that customer satisfaction should be the principal marketing activity of the firm is one such example.

The conviction in the efficacy of customer satisfaction is nearly universal. Roughly 90% of U.S. firms have customer satisfaction as a goal in their mission statement. More than 50,000 articles on customer satisfaction have been published in academic journals and business publications. Indeed, numerous books extol the necessity of relentlessly pursuing customer satisfaction.

But this core marketing concept has several profound weaknesses.

Customer Satisfaction Does Not Predict Repurchase

This is the elephant in the boardroom that marketing organizations typically ignore. Extensive research shows that the link between satisfaction and repurchase (much less loyalty) is tenuous at best and nonexistent at worst. In large-scale meta-analyses, the most favorable results show that customer satisfaction explains only 8% of repurchase behavior.

If this lack of correlation between satisfaction and repurchase is so well known, why do companies spend billions of dollars pursuing high levels of customer satisfaction? Several answers to this question exist, but the main reason is that a tantalizing connection can be found between satisfaction and a customer's reported intention to buy a product in the future. Unfortunately, a large correlation doesn't exist between what consumers say they plan to buy and what they actually purchase.

This seems counterintuitive. How can satisfied customers who say they plan to remain loyal not predict future success? From the last chapter, we know that much of the reason is because the habitual mind controls most of our behavior. The deep well where the majority of decisions are made lies behind an impenetrable veil. Not only are the habitual mind's workings unavailable for conscious scrutiny, but the conscious brain denies the extent of the habitual mind's control.

So when marketers ask customers if they are satisfied, the executive mind puffs up and starts thinking through the purchase, meal, or movie. This evaluation process is highly unnatural, but we think this is the way we always evaluate our experiences. If these same customers are then asked about future intention, they will consciously harmonize their intention with prior satisfaction judgments. However, their future behavior is still under the invisible influence of the habitual mind.

Satisfaction Is Based on Expectations

Marketers have discovered that ideas of value, positive regard, and reward are not highly correlated with the concept of customer satisfaction. Instead, satisfaction is conceived to be primarily a disconfirmation of expectations—essentially, it is an evaluation of whether a product did what the customer expected it to do.

Buyers form an expectation of how a product will perform before they purchase it. If the product underperforms on their expectations, dissatisfaction results. If the product simply performs as expected, customers report a neutral response. Only if expectations are exceeded do we see clear levels of customer satisfaction.

We can see this process in action by comparing eating at McDonald's to eating at an expensive French restaurant. If we don't have our food three minutes after walking into McDonald's, we get impatient. However, we expect to wait at a French restaurant for 10 or 15 minutes just to be seated, even if we booked a reservation six months in advance. Expectations are often unintentionally created. When McDonald's opened drive-through windows, customers expected the service to be quicker than service inside. What McDonald's developed as a convenience for the customer created an expectation that resulted in customer frustration.

Although it is logical to think that fulfilling a customer's expectations is important, the idea that those expectations must be exceeded presents a problem. If a product or service goes beyond customers' expectations, they will adjust their expectations accordingly. No one is thrilled by getting a Federal Express package on time—it is merely an expectation that was met. Marketers who want to continue satisfying a customer find themselves living Alice's dilemma: needing to run twice as fast just to stay in place.

You have probably seen signs in retail and service centers that proclaim "Our goal is to exceed your expectations!" Although ridiculous, the sign makes sense if you take seriously the generally-agreed-upon definition of customer satisfaction. Nordstrom faces the consequences of its vaunted customer service reputation. How is it possible to exceed expectations when customers expect so much?

Marketers pursuing the goal of customer satisfaction based on expectation face a dilemma. They must promise a lot to get a sale—but to create satisfaction, they must underpromise and overdeliver. Is it realistic to expect a company to continuously walk such a fine line?

Overall High Satisfaction Scores

Looking across all products and services in the United States, average customer satisfaction ranges 75–85 on a scale of 0–100. On most questionnaires, the highest-ranking score possible on the questionnaire gets the most responses. It's the ultimate grade inflation: Companies believe they are doing well, when, in fact, their performance is average.

Generally, high satisfaction scores further explain why satisfaction is not a good predictor of repurchase. Customers are saying that they are fine with most products and services they use. "Fine" in their minds is a score of approximately 85. Can marketers get higher scores? And if they do, will that lead to repurchase? The answer to both questions is a qualified yes. When customers report being "delighted," they display some level of loyalty. But "delight" has proved to be a quixotic measure that is difficult to obtain and even harder to maintain.

Do you realistically believe you can delight your customers every time they use your products or services? Numerous companies use delight as a customer service goal because of this research, but employees are hard pressed to know what will delight their customers.

Fully Explicated Satisfaction Judgments Are Rarely Made

Usually, people simply do not make satisfaction judgments about the products they use and the services they receive. When was the last time you thought about your brand of toothpaste, coffee, or soda? Most of our choices are not choices at all, but merely the execution of well-established habits, many that we made in childhood.

A great example of this comes from research conducted by the NPD Group examining what kids eat for breakfast. Harry Balzer, Vice President of NPD, studied the top-ten breakfast menu items mothers fed their children during two, two-year time frames: from 1985 to 1987, and from 2005 to 2007. Except for waffles being added in the most recent survey and fruit drinks dropping off the list, today's moms are feeding their kids the same things moms were 20 years ago. "It proves that the driving force in our lives, more than anything else, is our past," Balzer explained to me shortly after the report was released.

The list is the same, but it is not static. Waffle consumption increased 29 percent and yogurt increased 15 percent, but toast consumption decreased 20 percent and eggs dropped 12 percent. And, of course, brand market share during this time period has also shifted. But as Balzer notes, "Most of the foods eaten in this country are introduced to us by the age of five, and we spend the rest of our lives looking for variations of them."

When asked about the subject of habits and habitual control of customer behavior, Balzer's response was quick and blunt. "Of course habits control what we eat, what we buy, what we do. But our habits can act in contradictory ways. The breakfast habit would predict that what I ate yesterday would be the same thing I ate this morning. For dinner it would be the opposite. My habit is to eat something different tonight than I had for dinner last night."

Balzer went on to make a very important point: "Variety seeking is habitual. We love new." But just because customers try something new, does not mean they stick with it. "What companies think of as trends are actually fads working their way through the population." Even if they like the product they try as a novelty, they rarely include it in future habits. "Maybe one out of a hundred things we try while variety seeking actually becomes part of our habits."

The distinction between fads and trends is critical. Quaker Oats paid $1.7 billion for Snapple at the height of its popularity in 1993 and sold it for $300 million four years later. Quaker Oats' president and CEO both lost their jobs because of that deal.

Similarly, Coca-Cola is attempting to offset a persistent decline in carbonated beverage consumption (a trend) by launching new products and acquiring other beverage brands. It remains to be seen if categories such as vitamin water and energy drinks are fads or trends. If the former, Coke's investments might prove as questionable as Quaker Oats'.

Making a strong satisfaction judgment is much more the exception than the rule. Usually, we are simply getting the job done, whatever the job might be.

Becoming Your Customers' Habit

"That's a damn fine cup of coffee," special agent Dale Cooper observes in an early episode of the 1990s TV drama *Twin Peaks*. This line became memorable because it is so contrary to experience. We typically do not consciously pass satisfaction judgments on a cup of coffee—which brings us to Starbucks.

Ask CEO Howard Schultz why customers pay an average of more than $3 for a cup of Starbucks' coffee three times a week, and he will wax rhapsodic about the company's relationship with coffee growers, its emotional connection to customers, and its bond with partners (employees). But Starbucks' phenomenal success is arguably attributable to more mundane attributes.

The first factor in the company's creation and domination of the chain coffee store market is the role convenience plays in creating habits. Starbucks is the butt of many jokes relating to the proliferation of its stores, including the fake news announcement that a new Starbucks was being opened in the men's room of an existing Starbucks. A Starbucks even exists in China's Forbidden City. Yet the ease with which customers can find and get to Starbucks largely explains the company's success. Starbucks is willing to open a store across the street from an existing Starbucks if traffic pattern analysis justifies it. The typical logic of not wanting to cannibalize existing store sales is replaced by the knowledge that you sell a lot more coffee if you don't make customers cross the street to get it.

The other factor explaining the fanatical loyalty of its customers is that Starbucks' coffee contains a lot of caffeine, a drug noteworthy for being habit forming. Providing nearly ubiquitous access to one of our favorite addictions is a great business plan.

This leads to an alternative view of what our marketing goal should be: Instead of focusing on customer satisfaction, companies should be dedicated to customer habituation.

Customer satisfaction keeps organizations focused on the unreliable executive mind. By becoming your customers' habit, you are aligned with the power of the unconscious mind and focused on behavior instead of attitudes.

If you successfully become your customers' habit, the relationship is largely automatic. In a given context, your customers will use your product or service unconsciously. This does not mean ignoring the executive mind, but understanding where conscious decision making comes into play.

Customer habituation is a process that begins before acquisition and extends throughout the lifetime relationship of the customer. To take a customer away from a competitor, you must break the customer's existing habit. This means dislodging behavior from the unconscious mind and elevating it for executive review. Just because a behavior rises to conscious awareness does not guarantee that the customer will switch—simply that the power of repeat purchase has been interrupted. To get a shot at winning this customer, your offering must promise to deliver on the element that caused the habit to break.

An alternative acquisition strategy is to win a customer who is not currently using a product in a given category. The initial purchase is a process, not an event, typically described by hierarchy of effects models. Customers are posited to go through the following stages: awareness, interest, evaluation, trial, and purchase. Some models extend this to include satisfaction and repurchase. The Customer Habituation model extends this further to include repeat purchase and, eventually, habituation. The front end of this process is heavily loaded toward the executive mind, but the ultimate goal is to win the habitual mind.

Although you are trying to convince the executive mind to evaluate your product, you need to understand the rules that customer segments use for product selection. These rules, called heuristics, reside in the habitual mind. In general, customers pay relatively little attention to specific product features. Instead, they are looking for shortcuts, cues in the environment that enable them to automate decisions. Understanding how customers shop is essential if your product is even to be considered for selection.

When customers initially select a product, service, or store, this represents only the first step in becoming a habit. During the early stages of product familiarization, the executive mind is active and more likely to make conscious evaluations of performance. Being easy to work with and solving the customer's problems are essential. This enables the executive mind to begin turning over the decision to its habitual counterpart.

To form a habit, every facet of the experience plays a role. If any element creates a shock—pricing, product performance, customer service, even the packaging—it can interrupt the habit-forming process. If the conscious mind continues to be engaged, especially negatively, it can't automate repeat-purchase behavior.

To examine the implications of such an orientation, this section of the book updates the most basic marketing principles from a customer-habituation perspective. Whenever possible, we reference current marketing and management research and best practices, but the goal is to address the basic marketing education received either in business schools or from corporate education.

Although marketing has moved far beyond the Four P's (product, place, price, and promotion), we use this model as a lowest common denominator. The Four P's was immortalized by E. Jerome McCarthy's 1960 publication of *Basic Marketing*. Simply put, the 4 P's model provides an organizational structure for companies to create a plan to get products to the market. We also address the impact of habits on market research and the importance of the brand.

6

Habit and Marketing Management

The product component addresses the actual attributes of the product or service. For the sake of simplicity, the role of habit as it relates to the product follows a life cycle approach and takes the perspective of the product manager. Throughout this chapter, we use the term *product* in its broadest sense to mean a product, service, or bundle of products and services. This includes web-based offerings and online services.

The first chapter cited a dismal statistic that as much as 80% of new products fail or radically underperform expectations. Based on the habit research covered previously, it is clear that for a new product to succeed in a highly competitive marketplace, it must either create a new habit or replace an old one. In the next three sections on product design, product development, and product launch, we look at how current best practices often inadvertently lead to bleak results. Then we show how new products will have a far better chance if they are designed, developed, and introduced based on creating habitual use.

Habit and Product Design

Designing a product or service for the habitual mind requires a nontraditional approach. Each element, including physical layout, form factor, functionality, and intangibles such as service plans and warranties, impacts how well a product or service becomes habitual. In the design phase, the focus needs to be on the specific behaviors the user will perform. Decisions made at conceptualization have a disproportionately large impact on the product's life cycle. Seemingly innocuous decisions made in the early stages often sabotage an offering's future or, as with the iPod, position a product for market domination.

Marketers have long known that it is better to focus on a product's benefits than its features, but this mentality is often absent during design. Marketers who receive a product already designed or manufactured then attempt to translate its features into benefits. In designing a product for habitual use, benefits get baked in instead of painted on. However, a company's organizational structure can promote or inhibit this process.

Because product developers often do not know the end user very well, they tend to add features to make sure that all bases are covered. To leave something out that a customer might deem critical to purchase would then artificially shrink the market. Product managers often share in this belief and prefer to err on the side of including too many instead of too few product attributes.

The problem with this approach is that products and services become cluttered with features that customers don't use, making it more difficult to discover and use those features customers would find valuable. This dynamic is especially prevalent where the cost to include an additional feature is nominal, such as with electronics and software. The low variable cost makes it seem trivial to include one more feature. However, the resulting cost to the consumer might be exceedingly high, either because beneficial features are lost in the clutter or because complexity prevents habituation. From cell phones to PCs, most consumers use less than 10% of the features that come with their electronic devices. We see the same phenomenon in software and financial services: Users are so overwhelmed with options that they become intimidated.

Designing a product or service that leads to habit-forming behavior requires rethinking the development process. Designers must observe actual customers using the product in a natural context. Although feedback from customers is useful, it must be tempered by observation to account for parts of behavior outside executive control.

The actual design process must be guided by a habit-forming philosophy. To create a habit, either the product must be intuitive or users must be trained. Typically, users are unwilling to go through multiple steps to use a product unless the process is highly intuitive. Research on cell phone use shows that customers are unwilling to go beyond two clicks to access a function. This is similar to research on web site utilization and software applications. If the steps are seen as progressive, with one step logically leading to the next, users might be willing to follow them, but developers should err on the side of minimalism to create habits. Similarly, users might look at a manual when first using a product, but they typically don't read more than a few pages and rarely return to it. And, of course, many people don't even look at the manual.

Sometimes the nature of the task requires that a product design be complicated. In such cases, habits can still be formed but the customer requires training. For example, the QWERTY keyboard is hardly an intuitive layout for the alphabet, but we receive such extensive training with the interface that we can type a word a second without ever looking at the keys (actually, looking at the keys only slows you down). Many of us take typing in school, and we've translated the layout to smartphones and other devices.

However, the QWERTY layout is not optimally designed for speed or accuracy. Early typewriters had the keys used most frequently in the center of the keyboard, to speed typing. This led to the keys becoming jammed with the nearly simultaneous striking of vowels and the S and T keys. Spreading these keys around the keyboard slowed typing and reduced key jams. This design requirement basically disappeared when the word processor replaced the typewriter, but the power of our typing habits has proven nearly unbreakable. Several "superior" designs, such as the Dvorak keyboard patented in 1936, have been introduced and subsequently relegated to the new invention dustbin.

This doesn't mean that it is impossible for another text-based user interface to emerge—even one that is nonintuitive. Americans send more than a billion text messages a day, most using the number keypad on their cell phones. Triple tapping, or using a service called T9, wireless users all over the world have learned how to use this interface habitually. Through a combination of lightning-quick thumbs and innovative shorthand, those proficient in text messaging commonly average close to 40 words per minute.

These examples are given not to suggest that good design doesn't matter, but to illustrate that success comes from people using a product or service enough times that the habitual mind learns to use it automatically. Most product managers cannot count on schools teaching students how to use their products. Therefore, it is critical to focus extensive resources at the front end of product design and development.

If your product is for the consumer market, don't assume that customers will spend any time reading instruction manuals or even looking at the directions on the back of the package. Even complex products sold to corporations rarely include the level of training that can reliably be expected to create new habits. Designers and product managers must have clear behavioral outcomes in mind at the beginning if they are to have a reasonable chance of controlling their success.

To design products and services for rapid habit formation, developers must understand the context in which they will be used. Designers need to create products for rapid habituation by using not only human-centered design principles, but also task-centric design principles. They should minimize complexity in the interface, create feedback mechanisms so that the user can be trained quickly and reliably, and facilitate this process by creating mental models for the user.

Habits and Product Development

Taking a product from the drawing board and getting it ready for the market is a daunting process. Although the designers might have had a clear vision of a product's purpose, it is difficult for that vision to survive when it must go through an organization's silos, processes, and procedures. Not only do new products need to compete in the marketplace, but they must also compete internally for resources. This process often results in trade-offs that rob a product of its potential.

If a project manager takes a habit-forming view, then the product development process can prioritize around behavioral outcomes. Companies that consistently bring successful new products into the marketplace are able to bind what the product does to how a customer wants to get something done. This requires developing products based on a vision. Companies with a track record of consistently launching successful new products often have visionary leadership—high-level executives ensure that everybody shares the vision. Unfortunately for most organizations, their processes create so much inertia that the vision gets lost.

My cable company, one the nation's largest, spent millions to create a video-on-demand (VOD) service, enabling customers to view shows when they wanted and giving them controls similar to those on a DVD player. This represented a significant competitive advantage over satellite providers, who didn't have the bandwidth at that time to provide a similar service. To create the service, cable companies had to invest in vast server arrays to store and deliver the digital content, upgrade the two-way functionality of their networks, and work with hardware manufacturers to build the set-top boxes that would enable the service. It took years for VOD to go from the drawing boards to people's living rooms.

However, my particular cable service provider has created an absolutely terrible interface for this service. Customers have to navigate through 18 nonintuitive, text-based categories such as News & World, Searchlight, and Life & Home. Trying to find a specific program requires patience and determination.

Helping a friend locate the previous week's big game on his flat-panel TV required following these steps:

1. Push the dedicated VOD button on the remote.

2. Look through ten nonintuitive menu items and selecting Sports and Fitness.

3. Bypass the first page of ten menu selections and go to the second page. (We still have not seen anything that says "college" or "football.")

4. Try the Local Sports category, but face disappointment because this has only high school sports.

5. Go to the More Sports button—still no college football.

6. Out of frustration, click on the tab that has the name of cable company on it—eureka, college sports.

Although we had to go through a few more menus to get to the game we wanted, from that point on the choices were logical and relatively easy to follow.

Habits are created by repeating steps enough times to train the habitual mind. The more steps, the more repetitions are necessary for the neurons in the basal ganglia to record the patterns. The performance of the VOD system was sufficiently responsive to make the service habit forming, but the interface undermined all the effort and money invested. Only the most dedicated or bored viewer will go through this many steps, and it will never become habitual.

For product developers to build internal support, they typically focus on sales, revenue, or customer satisfaction. Instead, they need to articulate the behavioral goals the product is designed to create—a task much more difficult than it sounds. It is as hard for developers to break their habits as it is for customers to break theirs.

Organizations vary in their orientation to the marketplace:

• Operations focused

• Functionally focused

• Product focused

• Market focused

Companies often use some combination of these orientations, typically by vertically integrated silos. After an organizational structure is put in place, it develops policies, processes, and procedures that all products must navigate. Employees are placed in silos or boxes on an organizational chart, which creates its own culture and compensation. The folks in production are generally operations oriented, upper management is organized around functional responsibilities, and marketing is focused on the marketplace. In the 1930s, Procter & Gamble (P&G) developed the product management discipline to make sure that products made it through these processes efficiently. Product managers are essentially mini-CEOs, steering products through the organization's internal organizational maze and making sure that hand-offs between them are not dropped.

As discussed previously, the executive mind creates all these organizational structures as a way to break tasks into manageable chunks. Unfortunately, this process creates an intrinsic bias toward developing products for the executive mind, often at the expense of the habitual mind. It's hard to reconcile the need to create an organizational structure with the need to produce products that work with the unconscious mind. Out of this need has emerged the product champion, a person within the company who knows how to drive the processes to get a product to market without sacrificing the vision.

Although Steve Jobs plays this role at Apple, clearly no one did at my cable company. If an aspect of the iPhone or iMac violated Jobs's vision of the device, it was dumped or sent back to the drawing board. Clearly no one at the cable company said, "This interface defeats the whole idea. Fix it!"

To manage the process, everyone involved in product development must have a clear vision of what success looks like from a behavioral perspective. How frequently will the product be used, by whom, and in what context? Expressing developmental goals in behavioral terms can prevent obvious errors. Anyone using my cable company's VOD menu system would immediately recognize how difficult it would be to use habitually.

The second step is to understand the thresholds that determine a customer's usage. Thresholds can include quality, performance, usability, convenience, price, and other attributes. If a product misses on even one threshold, it can fail to become habitual because the executive mind continues to be engaged. This doesn't mean that more of something is necessarily better (except in the case of chocolate). Exceeding thresholds typically doesn't win you extra loyalty because the brain is simply trying to hand off a decision from the executive mind to the habitual mind. It's important to understand the performance/price threshold of each segment.

The product manager must also relentlessly ensure that everything comes together to fulfill the original goals of the product design process. Before the product is launched, all its constituent pieces need to be brought together to see if they create a coherent whole. This must be done using real customers in a natural setting. Simply showing a product to a customer or having a customer use a product for a short period in an artificial setting will not help a manager determine whether it has potential to be habit forming.

The Swiffer: Designed to Clean Up

In 1999, P&G introduced the Swiffer line of cleaners, creating a new product category that became one of the company's most successful launches of all time. But the inspiration for the Swiffer came five years before, when a group of designers took on the grimy job of watching people clean their floors.

Harry West came to the dirty floors of America via Cambridge University and MIT. The former professor with a Ph.D. in Robotics managed the team from Design Continuum, whose assignment was to help P&G replace the mop.

West explained that the key insights into the Swiffer's eventual design came from watching people get ready to clean their floors. "They were in old jeans and rubber gloves. This was clearly a dirty job." Because the designers observed actual consumers, they came away with the essence of an idea that they could not have gleaned from reading a research report.

"From the fall of 1994 to the spring of 1995, we went into people's homes and watched them clean their floors," West recalled. "There were teams from Continuum, P&G, and the advertising company going into people's homes for an hour. We talked with the homeowners, but not necessarily about floor cleaning. Mostly we watched."

From this experience, two things stood out. "The solution had to be quicker and cleaner for the floor, and it had to be quicker and cleaner for the consumer." When we got back to our offices in Boston, we intuitively came up with the solution—a diaper wipe on a stick.

"We spent a lot of time justifying why we thought this was such a good idea, but we knew we were on to something. We spent hours watching video we had taken of people cleaning their floors," West recalled. "If you just came here from Mars and had no reference point for what these people were doing, you wouldn't know if they were cleaning their floors or cleaning their mops. They spent equal time on both tasks."

In discussing the difficulty of uncovering habitual behavior in the design process, West stressed that Continuum prioritizes designers observing people in natural environments. "Let me set up the typical straw man approach. Market researchers are given an assignment, and they go about setting up their research approach. They collect data, both qualitative and quantitative. They document what they see in notes, charts, and graphs. They want to be smart about it, but they aren't designers. They are capturing only a tiny fraction of the information. And by codifying what they see, they are being very left-brain. Then they hand off their reports to the creative team, which has access to only a tiny fraction of information that the research team has."

West contrasts this approach with the process at Continuum. "Part of the reason we are successful is because we bridge the gap from consumer insight to either a product or a vision. By having the designers observing actual users, we capture the essence of a solution or a product."

I asked West how the essence of their idea for the Swiffer survived the product development process. He gave significant credit to Craig Wynett, who put the original teams together. "The assignment was based on the simple idea that there has to be a better way to clean the floor. By bringing in the ad agency and the people from P&G's hard-surface cleaning group, we were able to communicate much more effectively. They had seen what we had seen, so they could understand where we were coming from."

But Swiffer owes much of its success to another important insight from the Continuum team. For the folks at P&G to believe in the idea of a diaper wipe on a stick, they needed to see it. "In the spring of 1995, to communicate the idea, we made one." West went on to explain, "There was tremendous value in the prototype. I went back to P&G eight years later to do a presentation, and they still had the original one I brought to them that spring."

When P&G's product developers began the hard work toward commercialization, the prototype kept the essence of the idea front and center. West pointed out that having the ad agency involved provided the same benefit. The original ad company created prototype ads that preserved the marketing message as well. "Prototypes communicate so much more than a specification," West said.

When I asked him if he was happy with the result, West said he was delighted. He laughed and added another indicator of the power of the prototype. "There were some things we just threw into the prototype to make it work that ended up in the final product."

Product Launch: Creating Mental Models and Building Habits

Launching a product is similar to launching a rocket—you have to break the tremendous inertia that is holding a body at rest. Getting a product to be noticed in the cluttered and clamorous marketplace takes a coordinated effort among sales, marketing, and distribution. If it's a consumer product, launches might involve millions in advertising and heavy promotional spending. Business products typically launch with less fanfare, but instead have large-scale efforts directed at direct sales and customer education.

Successful launches grab the attention of the executive mind. Companies not only want their new products noticed; they also want potential customers to go through as much of the purchase process as possible—from awareness through evaluation and interest, all the way to trial. Although the launch process is focused on executive processes, success comes from positioning new product offerings globally to the habitual mind.

When companies talk about launching a new product, they can mean anything from a revolutionary new idea to a simple modification of a product they have been making for years. The rarest of "new" products are just that—new to the world, never before seen. When Dean Kamen introduced the Segway in 2001, it was truly a new-to-the-world invention. Less dramatic, but often just as challenging, is the product development that others offer but is new to the company. The decision to pursue these products can be reactive in response to a competitor or proactive in pursuit of market opportunities.

Less radical but still challenging is bringing out new products based on existing products, such as product line extensions. And at the low end of the innovation spectrum is "new and improved," in which a company is simply updating an existing product. Yet any change to an established product carries a profound risk—that changes will interrupt customers' habitual purchase behavior. The launch of New Coke is a cautionary tale to all brand managers.

These distinctions are important at the launch phase because we need to understand our customers' existing mental models for a product and a product category. Mental models are largely formed unconsciously and relate to two sets of neurons in the PFC: one that creates categories and one that creates rules. Positioning a product creates a type of mental map inside the customer's mind. The more richly a product connects to existing associations and emotions, the stronger the brand identification. Launching a new product becomes a balancing act between using customers' existing mental models so they can understand where to place a new product and simultaneously focusing on some level of differentiation.

The more "new" a product is, the more work must be done at the front end to create or modify a category in the brain to begin the habit-forming process. Commercialization for the Segway was difficult because it didn't compare to anything else. Conversely, the more a company's "new" product is perceived to be similar to existing products, the less it will stand out at launch. New products can also be positioned by what they are not.

The Baby Boom generation grew up in the back of station wagons and were damned if they were going to drive them as adults. When

Chrysler introduced the minivan in 1983, it provided the utility of the station wagon without the 1960s baggage. The Dodge Caravan was an instant hit, spawning a host of imitators. The minivan was the anti–station wagon.

However, a lot of fathers didn't want to be seen driving a minivan, which was tagged as the soccer mom vehicle. The SUV filled the resulting market opportunity. The SUV was the anti-minivan. In the world of male and female asymmetries, it's worth noting that the female brain experienced little, if any, reluctance to driving the beefiest SUVs Detroit puts out.

In marketing's relentless pursuit of new opportunities, most SUVs never left the road, paving the way for yet another alternative to the station wagon—the crossover. A cross between a car and an SUV, the new category is so nebulous that some manufacturers put them on car chassis and others use a pickup truck platform. Although crossovers have not seen the success of either minivans or SUVs, the green revolution might position these smaller vehicles in the consumer's mind as the right mix of size and gas economy.

Although the station wagon never went away, it largely faded from sight until the Dodge Magnum arrived in 2005. Combining the looks of a muscle car with slightly futuristic lines, this wagon was a hit with urban trendsetters and was even used in the science fiction move *The Island.* It's doubtful that the Magnum will create a new trend for station wagons, but it does show how playing off existing mental models creates endless market opportunities.

The successful launch of each subsequent generation of family vehicle was predicated on making a connection to preexisting models in the minds of customers. These mental models are both conscious and unconscious, tagged by emotions and retrieved by hundreds of cues in the environment.

The more unique a new product is to the market, the more money and time a company will need to spend building customers' mental models. But even modifications of existing products need to be positioned. Tremendous pressure exists to focus launches on either hype or dry appeals to the executive mind. However, neither approach will likely create the kind of mental models necessary to start a potential customer on the path of purchase and eventual habitual use.

Preparing for a new product to win the executive and habitual minds requires a more nuanced approach using narratives and metaphors. Through stories and analogies, new products can quickly stake a claim on the internal mental representations that will rapidly lead to behavioral changes.

Narratives can be highly effective by placing a new product in the context of a story. For example, when it absolutely, positively has to be there overnight, you should use FedEx. One of the immutable laws of the universe is that a task will expand to the time allotted it. The people at FedEx give us one more day to get things done, and the company's ads have consistently told this story.

A less effective narrative used in 2007 has Dr. Robert Jarvik explaining how he switched majors from architecture to medicine after his father had a heart attack. This led him to develop the first permanent artificial heart, which somehow makes him a credible spokesperson for Pfizer Pharmaceutical's cholesterol-lowering Lipitor. The narrative is good; unfortunately, it doesn't explain the product—just the spokesperson. (In 2008, Pfizer pulled the ads after they came under review by Congress.)

Narratives are useful because they provide a context, a way for customers to understand how a new product fits into the scheme of things. Stories are effective because they appeal powerfully to the way we understand the world. A story that involves us in how or why a new product comes to the marketplace can connect on multiple levels to both the executive and habitual minds.

Similarly, metaphors are valuable tools for complex products and services that involve intangibles. It's hard to explain the benefits of an insurance policy, but you can "Get a piece of the rock" with Prudential and "You're in good hands with Allstate." Metaphors are often overused when a company has difficulty articulating a product's value proposition.

At launch, metaphors can serve an essential role in helping a new product gain a foothold in a customer's mind. Consumers are aware of thousands of brands, making it difficult for a new brand to make an impression. A metaphor can link a product to existing positive feelings. However, if customers don't make the link, or if the product doesn't actually embody the attributes of the metaphor, the launch will fall flat. Insurance companies use geckos, whales, Snoopy, and stags in addition to good hands and the Rock of Gibraltar. But metaphors are successful only if they can connect the essence of the company to a specific trait.

Harry West of Continuum makes the point that when a good metaphor presents itself, it can do a great job of quickly explaining an idea. "But sometimes metaphors really get in the way. Don't waste a lot of time trying to create a metaphor. If there isn't a good one, don't try to force it."

The stakes at launch can be huge, the culmination of millions or even billions in R&D and production costs. AT&T and Verizon, the two largest U.S. phone companies, are in a protracted launch of advanced video services. To take customers away from the entrenched cable providers, the phone companies have spent billions upgrading their networks. However, because their network build-outs are progressing neighborhood by neighborhood, the companies cannot mount a nationwide advertising campaign. Further complicating matters, the companies have deployed different technologies.

Although executives think an ideal competitive situation is not having any, competitors are normally required to make a market. In extraordinarily rare circumstances, a single company educates the marketplace about new product categories. To justify their monumental investment, the phone companies have to offer something more than simply a third video-delivery platform.

Few things in the world are more habitual than watching television. The average American watches more than four hours a day. The remote control might as well be grafted to our hands. To succeed, Verizon and AT&T must take advantage of existing habits by providing a service that behaves similarly to cable. The real challenge is changing customers' category neurons so that they equate cool video services with companies historically associated with boring voice services.

Launch represents a critical time in the life of a product. Undoing a bad first impression is very difficult. Although it's important to create anticipation and excitement to overcome customers' indifference, the earliest messages set the stage for how the product is positioned and ultimately used.

Product managers need to focus not only on developing mental models, but also identifying what behaviors a customer must go through to arrive at purchase. However, the end goal is to introduce the product in such a way that it leads to long-term habitual use—think relationship instead of transaction. Although it's important to build anticipation and excitement to overcome the inertia of indifference with which customers typically view new products, do not sacrifice a long-term relationship for a quick sale.

Make sure you know the answers to these questions before launching a new product or service:

1. What behaviors will lead to a sale? For example, you might expect potential customers to check out the web site, read a brochure, come in for a trial, or watch an infomercial.

2. What are you doing to give the customer an incentive on each behavior? What reinforcements do you have in place that will make that behavior likely to occur?

3. Although launching a product necessarily involves the executive mind, what existing mental models are you using to tap into powerful unconscious mental models?

4. If your product is new to the world, how are you tapping into your customer's existing mental models?

Building Habits

Until this point, the focus has been on setting the stage in the customer's mind for the behaviors that precede purchase and use. The focus now turns to habit-forming product management—managing products and services so that customers use them habitually. In brief, most of our customers' shopping behavior is not consciously thought out, but is the result of established habits. But not all habits are the same. It is useful to think of two forms of habits: automatic habits and rule-based habits.

Automatic habits, such as Nielsen's shopping on autopilot, occur when a problem has been solved enough times that the executive mind can turn it over to the habitual mind. This occurs in stable conditions, such as when a customer shops at the same store or uses a familiar web site to book airline tickets. Think of habits as shortcuts customers take to keep their executive mind free to solve novel problems. An automatic repurchase habit might mean that a customer is loyal to your brand or, conversely, that the customer doesn't even give your brand a thought.

Rule-based habits, or heuristics, are those that rely on mental formulas to solve problems on the fly. A customer might have a rule that says "Don't buy extended warranties" or "When this brand is on sale, stock up." Most of the time, these rules are as unconscious as other habitual behaviors.

One of my marketing professors once described how he makes purchase decisions by drawing an S-shaped price-performance curve on a grease board. He pointed to the place where the line crested before heading off to the right, representing the point of highest value. "I shop here," he said proudly. Most of us aren't Indian-trained engineers with marketing Ph.D.s, so our heuristics are normally more obscure. But the point is important: We all develop strategies to speed us through purchase and usage decisions. After they are created, our heuristics give us one less complex thing to think about.

In real life, we use a combination of strategies to solve the countless decisions that confront us every day. Our executive and habitual minds are constantly trading off responsibilities, evaluating whether an automated response, a rule, or conscious problem solving is the best way to handle any given situation.

Almost every task combines these mental functions. Let's look at a common high-involvement purchase—buying a flat-panel television. Your starting point would likely be to go online to gather information. Automatically, you Google "flat-panel television" and the search returns millions of hits. Your conscious mind is engaged as you scan the first couple of pages but is quickly overwhelmed by the amount of information Google returns.

You then might employ a rule-based strategy, such as using the familiar web site like CNet or Consumer Reports. Searching on these sites returns more useful information, and your executive mind is once again engaged. Unfortunately, the technical distinctions between plasma and LCD make it difficult to understand which is better. You make it to the actual recommendations section, but so many caveats exist that no particular product, much less brand, stands out.

This experience often results in a decision not to purchase, but you are committed and decide to take your little bit of knowledge and numerous questions to a store and talk to a salesperson. This leads to another decision—which store to visit. Because you are undecided and are looking for information, you bypass the big box store and go to an electronics retailer that specializes in customer service.

Entering the store, you begin looking at the flat panels on display. You try to remember which display was supposed to have a sharper image, which had better contrast, and which was supposed to handle motion better, and whether you can tell the difference. When a salesperson approaches, you feel relieved to be able to discuss your quandary.

Although your conscious mind is attentive, you are unconsciously processing body language, facial expressions, and other cues to determine trustworthiness. Is he trying to sell you something or is he listening to what you want? You like the guy but still aren't sure if you trust him. However, after listening to you describe the room where the TV will reside, he not only suggests that you go with plasma, but he also recommends your favorite electronics brand. This triggers a rule-based decision, buying a trusted brand amid high levels of uncertainty.

Although most purchase or usage situations are not this involved, virtually all have the potential to activate both executive and habitual mental processes. Managing a product for habit formation requires a reformulation of our understanding of marketing and customer behavior.

Price Conscious

The price of a product or service is the other half of the brand promise—what the purchaser gives up to receive what the brand promises to deliver. Your price should reflect the brand promise—think of it as assurance pricing. Volvo's pricing should reflect the additional safety features in the car. If it didn't cost more, how safe could it be?

Competitive intensity typically predicates pricing decisions. In general, companies are torn between desire to raise prices to increase profits and reluctance to raise prices for fear of losing sales. However, by focusing on habit formation, marketers can use pricing as part of an overall strategy to shape long-term behaviors that resist competitive incursions.

The goal of pricing in the habit formation framework is to maximize profitability while keeping purchase and use decisions in automatic mode. If a customer has formed habitual use around a product, he or she factors the price into the behavior: A loyal Starbucks customer doesn't think about how much he's paying for his grande caramel macchiato. Customers who consciously attend to a product's price won't likely adapt habitual use.

Cell phones provide a clear example of this process. When wireless carriers charged strictly by the minute, customers restricted their usage. If you used your cell phone habitually, you ended up with a bill that would shock you back into conscious awareness. However, when carriers changed to monthly plans that included a bucket of minutes, cell phone use exploded.

If price is to become a nonissue, customers must go through a habit-forming process. For the initial transaction, the brand must establish a value commensurate with the price. This evaluation must be able to survive executive mind scrutiny. Ben & Jerry's goes to great lengths to position its company as socially responsible, to deflect attention away from the $3.50 it charges for a pint of ice cream. Although Mercedes-Benz has a well-established reputation as a prestige brand, it spends millions to educate customers about its great engineering and outstanding safety features. Purchase decisions might be largely based on emotion, but buyers require them to conform to some level of internal rationalization.

Shoppers don't make purchases in a vacuum, so the brand promise must support any variation from a customer's reference point for a category. Customers can automate a decision to pay more or less than the reference price if the brand's story supports it. Paying less for a generic brand can be habitual if the customer believes the cost difference is based on marketing expense, not quality. Yet most customers prefer well-known brands because their assurance of quality enables the customer to trust their promise. This benefit automates a decision to pay more.

Wal-Mart's success largely comes from the widely held belief that the giant retailer has the best prices. The low-price position is powerful because it provides a strong mechanism toward habitual behavior. Shoppers can confidently fill up their baskets at Wal-Mart, assured that they are getting the best prices available on whatever item they choose. The Arkansas-based retailer was able to leverage the strength of that automated shopping behavior when it expanded into groceries, successfully growing into a business far outside its perceived core competency.

On the other end of the spectrum are luxury and premium brands, whose high prices are as critical to their acceptance as low prices are to Wal-Mart's. From Rolex watches to Godiva chocolate, high prices guarantee the buyer a level of exclusivity that transcends a desire for quality. The fMRI scans show that well-known brands activate the same regions of the brain as self-identification, which powerfully suggests that the pricing story must conform to a customer's perception of self.

The appeal to pay more "because you're worth it" works because most of us believe that we are worth it. Others might view themselves as smart shoppers and need to feel that they got a good deal to link with self-image. To make accurate pricing decisions, companies need to understand the shopping heuristics of each segment and the context within which they are making the purchase. A regular Bud drinker might drink Dos Equis in a Mexican restaurant and take Heineken to a party.

One of the staples of maintaining a habitual relationship with a customer is to keep the repurchase process automatic. Few things elevate a purchase into executive awareness like a surprise on a bill. Customers can automate a purchase decision safely if they trust that the deal remains the same.

Market research long ago applied the psychological concept of the "just noticeable difference" to marketing-mix variables. Essentially, the idea is that a company can make small changes without altering the perception of the deal. Small price increases can escape notice, but if they exceed a customer's threshold of awareness, it can cause a backlash.

For years, companies have been trying to hide price increases by tacking on fees that are listed separately on the bill. From telecommunications companies to car rental agencies, organizations attempt to create psychological distance between price increases and the company. However, if the total bill is above the customer's threshold, the executive mind will examine it.

For purchase, use, and repurchase to become habitual, the price must be relegated to the unconscious. Any event that causes the executive mind to review the bill creates the possibility of defection. To achieve and maintain habitual use, pricing must be consistent with the brand promise. Price increases should be limited to either staying below customers' threshold of tolerance or be accompanied by a renewed value proposition.

Channels of Habituation

Habits are formed by convenience. You did not choose your dry cleaner because it had the best prices or best quality. You chose it because it is the one closest to your house or your office. This is why the place variable in the Four P's is the one most highly correlated with success.

To this point, habit formation has referred to a customer's use of a product or service. Equally essential is understanding how the shopping process is automated by looking at how customers navigate in space. Returning to the hippocampus from Chapter 2, "You Are of Two Minds (At Least)," this region of the brain combines multisensory information to create a mental map of the environment. Specific cells in this part of the brain learn to respond to specific locations. As with the rest of habit formation, learning comes through repetition. It takes a customer multiple trips to learn how to get to a store and multiple trips through a store to learn its layout.

Shoppers don't become customers until they learn to navigate a store or web site. In a conversation with an executive from a large retail chain, I discussed this process and the fact that it generally takes three visits to learn a store's layout. I speculated that the vast majority of people who come to her stores do so only once and don't return. Of those that come twice, most of them don't ever come back, even if they buy something. But shoppers that come three times become the customers that generate the vast majority of her sales. She stared at me silently for a moment, and then she asked me how I had obtained her company's proprietary data.

The predictability of shopper behavior comes from the physiological changes the brain undergoes as it unconsciously learns its environment. Until this learning is consolidated, a customer's attention is split between looking for items and understanding the store's layout. You don't become a customer until you can relegate navigating the store to the habitual mind. The number of times it takes to learn a store varies by how large and complicated the floor plan appears to the shopper.

Fortune Magazine rated Apple as the best retailer in America in 2007, citing its $4,000-per-square-foot revenues (compared to $2,600 for Tiffany and Co., and $930 for Best Buy). A large part of Apple's retail success comes from a radically simple approach to merchandizing. Instead of designing a store to sell computers, Jobs and company designed an environment that encourages people to interact with the emerging world of digital art and entertainment, from photography to video, to music. The result is a very open layout that the customer's hippocampus can quickly map, freeing the executive mind to experience and ultimately purchase.

Jobs continues to push the envelope with his stores, getting rid of the shelves that previously held software, even trying to get rid of the checkout counter. Sales associates check out customers with a portable credit card reader. The result is a store that gets rid of the clutter in the habitual mind so the executive mind can shop.

Most retailers can't adopt the Spartan approach that Apple's high-margin products enable, but they can understand the two-part process that must occur before a shopper can become a customer. By focusing on the behaviors that must occur to familiarize a potential customer with the physical layout of the store, retailers can significantly increase the proportion of shoppers who become loyal customers.

Positioning in the Retail Environment

According to my publisher, a book has somewhere between three and ten seconds to grab your attention in the bookstore. A single copy of a book that is spine out on a shelf with 30 other books in a section of several hundred books in a store of thousands of books is unlikely to be discovered. The odds that you found this book in a bookstore without prior knowledge are directly proportional to its placement and the number of copies available.

The science of merchandizing tells us the value of products being at eye level, the colors most likely to be noticed, and why items on end caps sell so well. These findings reflect both a customer's habits and sensory processing. As mentioned earlier, our senses evolved not to give us an accurate perception of the world, but to help us survive in a hostile environment. Consequently, our senses present a highly biased view of our surroundings, paying attention to change and motion. Our visual system also focuses on an object's edges, to better separate it from the background.

Books disappear in bookstores similar to sweaters in clothing stores and soup cans on grocery shelves. We find them because we are looking for them or something similar to them. The same goes for e-commerce sites that unfortunately repeat the mistakes of the real world in the virtual one. As we mentioned in the section on branding, every physical feature of the brand, product, and packaging can serve as a cue to automate the purchase process. However, if that feature is not part of a customer's existing purchase repertoire, it's more likely to simply become part of the background noise that the senses ignore.

This leads to promotion, in which companies attempt to communicate with customers to be on the lookout for their products and services.

Promoting Habits

Promotion is an odd marketing concept, encompassing a wide range of activities from advertising to sales promotions. Although it's hard to understand why a coupon would be in the same marketing category as a television commercial, the promotion P deals with anything that communicates with customers and potential customers. As previously noted, every component of the offer communicates something, but the promotion component of the marketing mix recognizes the responsibility of the firm to package its messages for customer consumption.

Hundreds of billions of dollars are spent annually trying to influence customer behavior. Unfortunately, many people believe that much, possibly most, of this money is flushed down the drain. "I know half of my advertising is wasted—I just don't know which half," John Wanamaker famously said more than a hundred years ago. Managers from small businesses to giant multinationals harbor the same sense of frustration when it comes to their promotional budgets.

This aggravation is largely a reaction to having been thwarted by customers' habitual processes for decades. Our senses are geared to ignore irrelevant stimuli, a process that is constantly refined as we learn about what is important in the environment. The first bill stuffer we see might get our attention, but after receiving hundreds of these little literary gems, we start tossing them in the trash without looking at them. The same goes for billboards, radio commercials, and magazine ads. Email was originally a very powerful tool for companies to communicate with their customers, until spam and phishing turned it toxic. Now we employ sophisticated software to help our senses filter out the junk. AOL's cute "You've got mail" audio announcement would drive us crazy with the hundreds of junk emails sent to each of us daily.

Adding to the complexity of promoting products is a radical transformation of promotion options. The Internet provides a platform of communications that advertisers found unimaginable just a few years ago with search, rich media, and now mobile options for reaching customers. Location-based services promise to radically alter the capability to combine promotional activities based on where a customer is in real time. The capability to send a coupon to a customer's cell phone when she's near a store or a coffee house or in a grocery store has marketers excited. We're still not sure what customers will think about this type of promotional intrusion.

To address the complexity of promotion, it's useful to break the concept into its constituent parts and address their implications to habit formation. Typically, promotion is broken into advertising, personal selling, sales promotion, public relations, and direct marketing. With the rise of the Internet (and IP distribution) and broadband wireless technology, several new categories of promotion have emerged, centering on search and email. In each instance, the focus is on generating the types of behavioral outcomes that will lead to specific goals.

Advertising

The advertising industry calls to mind a scene in Joseph Heller's *Catch-22* where Gen. P.P. Peckem is describing a new term he created.

A bomb pattern is a term I dreamed up just several weeks ago. It means nothing, but you'd be surprised at how rapidly it's caught on. Why, I've got all sorts of people convinced I think it's important for the bombs to explode close together and make a neat aerial photograph. There's one colonel in Pianosa who's hardly concerned anymore with whether he hits the target or not.

Advertisers trying to rise above the constant cacophony in the marketplace understandably focus intense attention on the creative aspect of the communication. However, similar to the colonel who was more focused on bomb patterns than hitting the target, ad agencies are often more intent on getting ads noticed than achieving behavioral outcomes. With advertisers paying for 4,500 messages per person per day, it's easy to understand that breaking through the clutter is perceived as job number one. But getting the ad noticed is not the same thing as creating a good ad.

Advertising has shaped our habits for generations. Advertising sufficiently offset the cost of newspapers to make them a daily ritual for more than a hundred years. Radio and television owe their very existence to a free broadcasting model, with advertisers picking up the tab for 24-hour access to music, news, movies, and serials. But the old advertising model is collapsing as habits shift in light of market fragmentation, technological innovation, and changing demographics.

As late as the mid-1970s, an ad agency could deliver the vast majority of American eyeballs by simply advertising on three nationwide networks during primetime, the three-hour block of television that turned us into couch potatoes. Newspapers reliably provided access to local markets, informing customers of sales, store openings, and classified ads. And radio stations came in two basic flavors, rock and roll and country, making it easy to reach the vast majority of the Baby Boom generation by buying some local drive time spots. However, our media consumption habits are going through a revolutionary change, and advertisers are desperately trying to figure out this new and alien landscape.

Michael Irvine is on the front line of the battlefield for the next generation of habits. A vice president of sales for ABC since 1985, he has seen his job go from cushy to chaotic. "It used to be simple. There was always a greater demand for our inventory (commercial air time) than supply. One agency would do everything from creation to media buying." Irvine is responsible for selling ad time on the local TV stations ABC owns, including L.A., San Francisco, and Houston—a job that has become much more complicated in the past few years.

When Irvine started with ABC (at the local Detroit affiliate in 1974), television was tremendously influential. For example, Miller Brewing launched Miller Lite in 1975 with its famous "Great taste/Less filling" television campaign that introduced America to the notion of low-cal beer. The launch was so successful that Miller rapidly grew to take over the number two market share position behind industry leader Anheuser-Busch, and the light beer category became the largest-selling beer segment in the United States in 1992. That kind of success is hard to come by in today's world of hundreds of cable channels, DVDs, the Internet, game stations, video-on-demand, and IP distribution of video.

"Instead of just selling one channel on 10 stations, now we've got digital channels, regional sports channels, and our web sites. I'm selling 71 different products plus combinations of products," Irvine explained, the frustration clear in his voice. "We might get four million unique visitors to a local station's web site a month, but advertisers are looking for sites that can do that in a week or a couple of days." Adding to his challenges, Nielsen, the bible of television ratings, changed its rating system. When I asked Irvine about the new system and impacts of personal video recorders such as TiVo, his response was colorful, to say the least.

After three or four minutes of invective, Irvine presented a picture of just how much advertising is changing. "We used to sell ad time based on theories of recency, reach, and frequency—the number of times you need to see an ad or whether you're in the market for a product. You never knew when somebody might be in the market for a car, so you advertised consistently. But now, you've got companies who have access to a lot more information wanting to change their media buys in response to what happened yesterday. And you're making promises about what you will deliver based on somebody punching in a code every 15 minutes. It's crazy, but that's our business now."

The inexorable link between advertising approaches and customer behavior is similar to a dog chasing its tail. For decades, we have awaited the fall for new shows, deciding which would become part of our routine for the next year by the end of September. Networks capitalize on this future revenue by getting advertisers to commit billions on next year's shows in a process called the upfronts, in which media planners play roulette by placing bets on next year's shows.

My conversations with Irvine took place during the writer's strike of 2007–2008, a turning point in the transformation of the content industry. We discussed how the timing of the strike would impact habits not only for the next season, but also for the foreseeable future. "Network executives rely on the upfronts so they'll know how much to spend on shows and the number of rewrites they can afford." Irvine pointed out that reality shows have much lower budgets and that the strike would tilt executives toward ordering more unscripted programming. The power of habit is not limited to customers. Network executives, writers, actors, and media buyers are guided by the way they made decisions in the past. Indeed, much of the writer's strike was an attempt to extend the status quo into the revolutionary world of digital media.

Although Irvine focused on changes in the behavior of advertisers, I pointed out that the risk could be much worse. Habits build up their own inertia—the more inertia, the greater the perturbation necessary to dislodge the behavior. Although it's shrinking, the major networks still control the largest percentage of audience viewing. Disrupting the traditional fall lineups will inevitably change the behavior of millions of viewers in unpredictable ways that are unlikely to be beneficial to the networks. As the baseball strike disrupted our sports habits for years, the writers might be killing the goose who lays the golden egg not only for themselves, but also for the networks.

It's worth noting that WPP's GroupM unit, the world's largest buyer of media, predicts that Internet advertising will surpass television advertising in Sweden, the United Kingdom, and Denmark during 2008. This shift in advertising spending reflects the underlying seismic shift taking place in how people are accessing information.

Advertising agencies have been navigating these changes for more than a decade, sometimes accelerating the process and other times desperately trying to hold them back. Eric, a media planner for a large agency, talked with me about the state of the industry and how his role integrates media into people's lives.

"The jig is up on advertising—people are on to us," Eric told me. "We can't approach the audience the way we used to." In response to my question about changing media habits, he agreed that the alteration is happening at the DNA level. "There is a new dynamic in the way people view advertising and new dynamics of media. It is totally unrealistic to expect the audience to make an extra effort to get your message."

Viewing customers as an audience is critical, Eric explained. "We have a responsibility to entertain and inform as well as communicate a message." If advertising does not create value for the viewer, it will not break through the brain's filtering mechanism. "We are focused on how to use media more coherently with the message. We're not looking at simply what we can do, but what we should do."

Eric agreed with the idea that the biggest challenges advertising faces is the customer's defense mechanisms against the sheer volume of advertising. "Agencies disaggregated message, media, and placement functions 15 years ago, and maybe that's been the problem. The creative area might have a great visual, but the placement people are just concerned with how many places they can put it, not whether the ad really works there. They're not really thinking about the consumer experience."

And the integration of media and message based on the audience experience has the best opportunity to rise above the cluttered media landscape. Similar to the deal inherent in the brand promise, advertisers need to also understand the deals they are making with customers. I get to watch TV and listen to the radio for free as long as I accept advertising. If I want to avoid the commercials, I can pay for the content. But if the advertising becomes too intrusive, I'll bypass it with TiVo, Netflix, satellite radio, or my iPod. If advertising is informative, entertaining, or making something I want free, it's a good deal. And if it's just clutter, I have a mind that has evolved over millions of years designed specifically to ignore it.

I asked Eric about the challenges of media planning in these times of enormous change in traditional media and the emergence of the Internet and mobile advertising. "We do a lot of TV because a lot of people still watch TV, and it's a great medium for our messages. We also use magazines because they still have a large readership. Yes, traditional media continues to lose customers, but we still use it to reach the bulk of the market. But the digital world opens up important possibilities about how we connect to and share information."

Eric explained that, regardless of the chaos of the times, "The best way to tell the story is as if we were simply showing the product to a friend." For this to be credible, it helps tremendously if the advertiser actually believes in the product. "There is a real problem when the ad reality does not meet the product reality." He quoted a line that strikes him as particularly appropriate: "Ad budgets are attached to a lot of mediocre thinking."

Marketers believe that the most powerful form of advertising is word of mouth (WOM), a contention that has a lot of research to back it up. Unfortunately, by definition, WOM is not advertising because no one pays for the message. And that's why it's so effective. When someone is trying to sell us something, we automatically discount the message. But if a friend or someone we identify with tells us about a product, a restaurant, or a movie, we listen. Our friend's recommendation bypasses our ad defense mechanisms and the skepticism we reserve for anyone trying to sell us something.

Ad agencies have struggled for years to capture the power of WOM, and they see tremendous potential in what is loosely called Web 2.0, the world of social networking. Blogs, web sites, MySpace, Facebook, IM, chat, and text messaging have eliminated the space and time constraints of human communications. However, in attempting to seize these new opportunities, agencies risk committing the same mistakes that have gotten them ignored in the past.

Customers want to shop efficiently and effectively, and advertising can help them achieve that goal. But if advertisers cheat, lie, or abuse customers by wasting their time, they sow the seeds of their own irrelevance. The Web 2.0 phenomenon has tempted numerous companies, PR firms, and ad agencies to pretend they are community members in an effort to sway online public opinion. Most of us are poor liars. We fail to make eye contact, our respiration increases, and we fidget. And most of us can tell when we are being lied to because of these same behaviors. A generation brought up on the Internet, IM, and text messaging spots these phonies just as quickly online as we do face to face. Not only does this make the target audience mad, but it also makes the offending company look clueless and dishonest.

Trust is essential to becoming part of customers' habitual behavior. A lack of trust guarantees that the person, product, service, or company remains under constant, conscious scrutiny by the executive mind. The allure of the digital universe beckons irresistibly because it provides a cheap, quick, effective means of communicating with targeted segments where they live. But this is a double-edged sword because anything seen as illegitimate will be instantly exposed and universally vilified.

Customers are constantly interacting with advertising on both conscious and unconscious levels. Accept this as fact: If you are intentionally dishonest in your promotional activities, what you lose will be far greater than whatever you hoped to gain.

The marketplace operates on a perception of fairness and honesty, and even when companies aren't being dishonest, their behavior can still violate their customers' unwritten code of conduct. In 2007, Facebook attempted to leverage its customer base by launching an advertising program called Beacon, which tracked purchases made by its 59 million users. This move created an immediate backlash based on privacy concerns, and the company's founder, Mark Zuckerberg, yanked the program and issued a public apology.

As discussed earlier, our emotions powerfully influence our beliefs, attitudes, and memories. Crafting ad campaigns to connect positive emotions to a brand or company is a primary goal of most advertising. Just as the vision of a product might not survive the product development process, a great product message can be tarnished by others' decisions within the company that are totally unrelated to your brand.

Dove soap launched one of the most successful Internet-based viral marketing campaigns with the release of a short video entitled *Evolution.* In fast forward, we see an attractive woman preparing for a photo shoot. Using her face and hair as canvas, an army of makeup artists transforms the woman to near perfection for the photographer's lenses. The resulting photograph is not simply retouched, but digitally altered to transform the already beautiful image into impossible perfection. The tag line, "No wonder our perception of beauty is distorted," captures the irrational quest for unattainable beauty that women around the world feel as a result of Madison Avenue and Hollywood's relentless presentation of surgically and digitally altered 19-year-old girls as role models for our daughters. Branded as Dove's Campaign for Real Beauty, the company launched a web site providing resources for women, even creating the "Dove self-esteem fund," to develop and distribute resources to broaden the definition of beauty.

Dove had hit a home run. The campaign was a hit with women and the press. Only one problem existed. Another clever alternative campaign was running wild on the Web. Axe body gel created "The World's Dirtiest Film" campaign that boasted great Web 2.0 credentials. It combined professionally developed video with user-generated content, was hooked up with Facebook and www.collegehumor.com, and featured eternally adolescent David Spade as its host. Aimed at young men, the video presented women in exactly the exploitive way that Dove's campaign for real beauty railed against. Unfortunately for the Real Beauty campaign, Unilever owns both brands: Axe and Dove.

Both campaigns benefited from the collaborative nature of Web 2.0, but that same power was turned against the company. With ironic genius, filmmaker Rye Clifton transposed the images from the Axe film onto another video from the Dove campaign that showed a young girl being assaulted by sexually charged images from advertising, TV, and film. Clifton replaced the powerful Dove message, "Talk to your daughter before the beauty industry does," with "Talk to your daughter before Unilever does." A petition to Unilever CEO pointed out the hypocrisy and challenged the company to stop the exploitation by yanking the Axe ads. A Unilever executive pointed out that the Axe ads were a spoof of the mating game, but Clifton's film, which has been viewed more than 100,000 times, makes that contention seem less credible.

The audience's unconscious mind picks up on cues invisible to the executive mind that creates the messages. The best path for companies and their ad agencies is to remember the brand promise.

Anything you do that breaks the promise or alters the deal will keep the purchase decision under executive review. And the global knowledge engine serves as a gigantic executive mind, exposing any hypocrisy and mocking any pretense.

The advertising industry has long sought to reduce its waste by targeting its messages to the segments most likely to buy a particular brand. It's much more efficient to sell golf clubs on the Golf Channel than on MTV. From mailing lists to behavioral targeting, advertising has greatly improved its ability to focus its investment. Eric laments what he calls "the loss of serendipity," in which messages are targeted so scientifically that they can't be discovered by groups beyond the limited vision of the media planners.

From a habit-forming perspective, advertising needs to facilitate specific behavioral goals based on one of three objectives: habit creation, habit maintenance, or habit breaking.

Habit creation means focusing advertising on getting new customers to try a product or getting existing customers to use a product habitually. From the perspective of the hierarchy of effects, advertising should be moving a potential customer from awareness to trial. Image advertising serves a limited function in creating awareness. Research from various disciplines indicates that customers will have a more favorable impression of familiar versus unfamiliar names. This partly explains why scandal-ridden politicians are often re-elected; voters recognize the name without necessarily knowing why.

But awareness is not enough. We are aware of thousands of brands, and most of them fail to cause any reaction. For a brand to become part of a behavioral repertoire, advertising needs to take customers to a state of mental readiness in which they are actively evaluating the product or service. Getting a potential customer to take the step from passive to active mental effort requires engagement—a connection to the message.

Variety seeking is a habit. Advertising can be very effective at getting people to try the barbecue chicken pizza and the mango iced tea, but few of these products will be anything but a one-night stand. For advertising to help a brand become a habit instead of a fad, it needs to facilitate shortcuts in the customer's mind.

In 1978, the International Ladies Garment Weavers Union (ILGWU) began an ad campaign encouraging shoppers to "Look for the Union Label." The commercial was decidedly low tech in terms of production values, with real union members singing marginally off key. Although the commercial ran only 60 times from 1978 to 1985, it was highly effective because it took an emotional appeal, supporting American workers, and tied that to a behavior, looking for the union label when buying clothes. The commercial's message was not "Try clothes made by union workers and you'll be impressed by their quality." The message was designed to shape shopping habits, connecting an emotional appeal to a behavioral shortcut. Looking for the union label became a habit for some customers.

The power of advertising to maintain and strengthen the habits of existing customers is far greater than its ability to persuade noncustomers to try a product. Seeing an advertisement in a magazine or on a billboard for your brand reinforces your choice. Similarly, seeing a product you already own used in new ways can create an immediate trial opportunity. Marketers often neglect reinforcing behavior because they are pressured to acquire new customers, often at the expense of their existing, and profitable, current customers.

Marketers have debated how many ad exposures are necessary to communicate a message. A companion debate surrounds the importance of timing to the exposure. Still another debate centers on the saliency of an ad. From the habit forming perspective, we can see the role of advertising for habit maintenance differently.

Habit formation is a multiple-step process in which a behavior is automated through repetition and reinforcement, and cues (any stimuli associated with the behavior) trigger the response. Advertising can facilitate this process by providing the educational component to begin usage. But ads are far more powerful by creating cues in the environment to activate behavior. Billboards for fast-food restaurants provide a good example.

Chick Fil-A's long-running "Eat More Chikin" ad campaign combines amusing commercials of cows encouraging us to substitute chicken sandwiches for hamburgers with eye-catching three-dimensional billboards. The humor, consistency, and three-dimensional approach make the cows' outdoor ad an exceptionally effective cue.

The most difficult job for advertising is to take a customer away from a competitor. You are working against established habits and must overcome the inertia related to prior behaviors. This means the ad must somehow dislodge the behavior from the habitual mind and elevate it to executive mind review. The difficulty in this approach is that habits are often executed so fast that the executive mind remains unaware of the process.

Advertising to take customers away from competitors has a better chance of success if events occurring in the marketplace are already getting customers to think about their current brand. New product introductions, new model years, and even updates of existing products all have a chance at getting a customer to move an automated decision up for executive review, even if only briefly. Even if the competitor is bringing out a new and improved model, it means that existing customers are consciously evaluating their current brand. And, of course, if the competitor makes a publicly visible mistake, your ads have a far greater chance of being attended to.

To facilitate habit formation, advertising needs to break down the behaviors that lead to purchase and repeated use. This means first understanding your potential customers' shopping heuristics. Do they use web sites, ads in magazines, or newspapers to get information on this product category? Is the product high or low involvement? How does the advertising campaign move the customer toward trial? By understanding your customers' and potential customers' existing habits, your advertising can facilitate instead of fight entrenched behavior.

Also, advertising must consistently link to specific behaviors. Advertising typically does not cause a purchase, but it can take a potential customer from awareness to interest and evaluation. Ultimately, advertising should get a customer to want to try a product, such as taking a car for a test drive or visiting the web site to view the trailer of a new movie. Ads that stop at attitude formation are not cost-justified.

What is the role of advertising for products that are already used habitually? Why does Coke spend so much time advertising if the vast majority of its customers are already executing incredibly powerful scripts? Clearly, value exists in providing a cue for purchase and also in reinforcing a purchase. Advertising also helps maintain relationships with distribution channels.

In reality, most of us can't tell the difference between Coke and Pepsi, or Miller and Bud in blind taste tests. (Oh, of course *you* can. I'm talking about the vast majority of other people.) The real story behind the New Coke debacle is that the market leader should not mess with people's habits. Coke had changed its secret formula before (most notably switching from sugar to corn syrup); they just didn't tell anybody. But New Coke forced the issue into our executive minds. The backlash was simply customer frustration at having to consciously consider a decision long ago relegated to habit.

Although customers prefer to buy brands they are aware of, the experiences associated with a brand are far more powerful than any advertising message. Advertising needs to facilitate a process that leads to and maintains habitual product use.

Personal Selling

Salespeople are in a unique position to facilitate a purchase by working with customers' habitual and executive minds. Personal selling can be an expensive but highly effective means of conveying the company's offer directly to a customer. A salesperson can use the vast array of human abilities to shape the deal and persuade the customer. However, customers have developed equally complex scripts to handle the sales pitch. Although I can't prove it, I'm sure the word *skepticism* originated as a response to an egregiously dishonest salesman.

The feedback mechanisms between customer and salesperson engage the conscious processing of the PFC, the emotional component of the amygdala, and the habitual processes of the basal ganglia. Although the customer might be consciously focusing on the offer, he or she is also unconsciously evaluating the salesperson for trustworthiness, as well as accessing a variety of shopping scripts. The salesperson is performing the same process in reverse, consciously and unconsciously analyzing the thousands of verbal and nonverbal cues the customer puts out while considering a purchase

Salespeople are weird. They don't seem to quite fit into the organization. It's almost as if they are working for themselves. They are. Commissioned salespeople are paid based on their performance, so their training is based on what works in the real world. This built-in feedback mechanism drives the salesperson's behavior, often to the detriment of the firm.

The mind of the salesperson is learning the same way the customer learns, evaluating not only immediate feedback, but also outcomes. A good salesperson becomes as expert at reading people as a well-trained therapist. A pushy salesperson is one who is not reading, or at least not respecting, the messages the customer is sending. But at some point, this technique worked for the salesperson, thereby reinforcing the behavior.

In collecting data from electronics stores for six months, I witnessed numerous excellent salesmen, but no women sales associates worked at any of the three stores where I collected data. The electronics industry was notoriously male dominated, providing a good example of how salespeople learn from their environment. The marketing director, a sharp, middle-aged woman who worked relentlessly with the all-male sales force, spent significant time with me explaining the abilities and limitations of her team.

"The guys are, in general, very good, but they don't know how to listen to women," she explained to me. "A woman will come in and specifically ask for a rack audio system, and the salesman will invariably try to talk her into buying separate components. The sales guy thinks he's doing her a favor because he's trying to get her the best sound for her money. But she's more concerned with how it's going to look in her living room and how easy it's going to be to put together." Normally, a commissioned salesperson is highly responsive to customer feedback, especially if it signals a "no sale" decision. But because the store's male-dominated culture is reinforcing the salesman, he's not picking up on the customer's cues.

Business-to-business (B2B) sales professionals understand the basic concept of this book—make the rebuy decision automatic. The last thing you want to hear from an existing customer is that she is initiating a request for proposal (RFP). The RFP from an existing customer is the B2B equivalent of purchase behavior being elevated from the habitual to the executive mind for review. Even if you maintain the account, the RFP process requires a lot of uncompensated work and usually results in lower margins and lower commissions.

For a salesperson to create a long-term relationship, whether in the B2B or consumer environment, it's similar to building a relationship based on the brand. The salesperson should develop his or her unique brand promise and clearly communicate it to customers and potential customers. As with the brand, a broken promise results in the customer keeping the purchase decision and continuous use of the product in the executive mind. Conversely, after trust is built, customers will come to rely on a salesperson's judgment.

The ultimate goal of the salesperson is to become a trusted advisor and consultant. Two principles of trust exist: honesty and competency. Typically, trust forms over time with repeated interactions. Salespeople motivated by the short-term prospect of an immediate sale often communicate a message of dishonesty or incompetence, even if they are making a recommendation that is in the customer's best interest.

Personal selling is an expensive but effective method of moving customers to purchase by appealing to both the habitual and executive minds. While the customer's executive mind can ask questions and process the salesperson's responses, the unconscious mind is working to determine trustworthiness. Salespeople should work to understand the shopping heuristics of their customers.

In personal selling, whether an SAP installation for a multinational or a refrigerator to a couple with three kids, the salesperson is selling him- or herself. For the buyer, trusting a salesperson can greatly simplify the purchase experience. The distrust we have in general for salespeople comes at a significant cost to us. We are forced to take on more effort to make sure we are not taken advantage of.

Salespeople are sorely tempted to take advantage of information asymmetries (they know a lot more than the customer about the product and its actual costs) to make a sale or maximize commissions. This leads to a transaction mindset, and many salespeople make a good living with this tactic. But this mindset turns the customer into an adversary because winning exacts a cost that lasts long after the sale. Salespeople train their customers to either trust or distrust them, impacting not only current but future sales.

Sales Promotion

In many ways, sales promotions have been impacting customers' habits for decades. Sales promotions are marketing activities that provide extra value to the sales force, distributors, or the ultimate consumer to stimulate immediate sales. Sales promotions are highly effective because they can trigger automated scripts that customers use to shop or break down established habits. However, sales promotions often result in customers learning to expect a promotion, creating deal-sensitive purchase behavior.

Sales promotions can be seen as push, getting products into distribution channels, or pull, getting end-use customers to go looking for the product. Under both conditions, companies are sweetening the pot to stimulate behavior, but in doing so, they risk changing the perception of the deal.

Sales promotions represent the behavioral fine-tuning large businesses need to balance reality against projections. If it's the end of winter and you have 10,000 unsold overcoats, it makes sense to try to get rid of them. The profit you hoped to make on them is a dream long gone, and your priority has shifted to offsetting potential losses. The cost of warehousing the coats for another season is prohibitive, and styles are likely to change in the interim. You are feeling the pressure, and every day you delay a decision makes your position that much weaker.

A trade-oriented promotion might be offering a deal to an existing distributor if he would take all the coats. You might even agree to throw in co-op advertising dollars. Conversely, you might rely on a consumer-oriented sales promotion, such as coupons offering a buy-one-get-one-free deal, or you might have a contest in which one lucky winner gets a trip to Alaska to show how well the coats work.

Sales promotions have grown over the years to eclipse the money spent on advertising. This has happened for a very powerful reason—sales promotions are working with the habitual mind and advertising is often working against it. A consumer-directed sales promotion is designed to get an immediate reaction from the customer. Through trial and error, companies learn how to craft these promotions to trigger a response.

The brain's automatic-response systems can learn to automate highly complex behaviors. The effectiveness of sales promotions is related to our established behavioral responses to events in the environment. When customers shop, they are in one of three states we have discussed. They can be on autopilot, relying on cues in the environment to activate habitual responses; they might be using heuristics, relying on simple rules to simplify decision making; or they might be consciously evaluating choices, engaging the executive mind to process a deal or consider the options. Let's look at how sales promotions can impact these three states.

When shopping on autopilot, sales promotions cue stored behaviors. Special point-of-purchase displays break the brand out from the background, which can activate a cue. Similarly, coupons can be used like a shopping list, guiding a customer through the store to specific books or televisions. In many ways, sales promotions are a reaction to the clutter created by the marketplace. The massive proliferation of products makes it hard for any one brand to stand out, forcing companies to go to extreme measures just to get noticed.

Promotional activity can also work into a customer's heuristics—indeed, sales promotions often create our heuristics. For example, people who consider themselves smart shoppers rely on deals to reinforce their self-image. To a smaller degree, a customer might become deal sensitive after repeated presentations of an offer. Coupons can easily reduce the cost of a box of cereal by 25% to 50%, a substantial savings for a family with a large grocery bill. If a customer periodically receives coupons for a preferred cereal, that customer might develop a script that says "Wait for coupon before buying cereal." Unwittingly, the promotion manager has created a new segment of the marketplace: the deal-prone customer. Companies and stores have tried to break this group of their addiction by promoting everyday low prices, but that doesn't cue the customer to buy a specific brand.

Promotions are often used as part of a product-awareness campaign to arouse the attention of the executive mind. Building product awareness is one of the main goals of sales promotions, a way to announce to the highly resistant conscious part of your brain that something new might be of interest. Successful campaigns can create sufficient buzz to take a customer from awareness all the way to trial.

But in the words of Harry Balzer, "Variety seeking is a habit." A sales promotion for building awareness can be effective in the long term only if it gets people to use a product repeatedly. Otherwise, these efforts will make a lot of noise, possibly even significant sales, but will not result in long-term success. A good example is Zima, the Coors malt-based alternative to wine coolers. Launched in 1994 with $50 million in marketing and promotional dollars, the campaign was so successful that nearly half of the alcohol-drinking American public tried it—once.

Sales promotions are effective because they work with the dinosaur brain and the executive brain. They can work with habits or disrupt them. Successful consumer-oriented sales promotions overcome the noise in the environment or work with the cues used by the habitual mind.

Trade-oriented promotions work much the same way, disrupting the automatic rebuy processes by creating attractive deals. Whether that means cooperative advertising dollars, price breaks, or cash for placement, sales promotions get the corporate buyer to buy more.

However, sales promotions have a dark side. When used proactively, they can advance the brand's strategic positioning. But when they are used reactively, they often undermine the brand's value proposition.

When car manufacturers began offering 0% financing, new car sales spiked. However, when the financing stopped, sales slowed.

Customers' perception of the deal had changed, if not permanently, at least for several years. Although managers instinctively understand this risk, they talk themselves into these types of promotions to address current problems.

Similarly, exclusive brands that dump excess inventory by using discount chains to move last year's goods can see years of a product's positioning eroded overnight. An exclusive brand that is available at a discount store is no longer exclusive.

Sales promotions to channel partners can have the same effect— buyers become deal conscious. Instead of adhering to traditional arrangements, everyone along the distribution chain enters into deal mode.

Sales promotions have grown over the years in direct relationship to their effectiveness. Because sales promotions are directed at driving specific behavior, these types of marketing efforts often prefer them to the indirect approach of advertising. However, sales promotions can have nasty side effects if they undermine the brand promise. Managers must evaluate potential alterations to the perception of the deal, not only on the brand, but on the company as well.

Public Relations

Public relations (PR) needs some good public relations. Viewed by many as the last refuge of scoundrels, PR is grossly misunderstood by the general public. As such, the potential of PR to help position the brand positively in the customer's habitual and executive minds is often neglected.

PR has several components that can effectively work with the rest of a marketing campaign to build a positive brand or company image. In general, PR seeks to create a positive impression of an organization or a product with the public. To do this, PR works with the media and often provides information to reporters, even to the point of writing entire articles for newspaper and magazines and creating video for television broadcasts. Because these messages are not paid for, they are embedded in news stories when they are picked up, which improves credibility. Most important, such presentations sneak past our well-honed ad defense system. This is part of PR's PR problem—it seems sneaky.

PR can be proactive or reactive. Proactive PR sets out to shape public opinion through managing relationships with various media, making corporate spokespeople readily available, and creating strategies to keep brands publicly visible. The Ronald McDonald House, sponsorship of museums and zoos, and other forms of public charity help companies appear to be good corporate citizens. When this strategy succeeds, the company's name is associated with positive feelings inside the habitual mind.

Reactive PR is damage control. Crises, whether the responsibility of the company or not, can undo years of brand positioning. From the Tylenol-tampering tragedy to the *Exxon Valdez* catastrophe, a single event can break the bonds of trust between a company and the public. A rapid and forceful reaction is required to reassure the marketplace that the company recognizes the scope of the problem and is doing everything possible to rectify the situation. The goal is to return the brand to the precrisis position in the customers' mental perceptual map. However, if the company gives the impression that the effort is merely PR, the backlash can be fierce. The worst case is when a company representative attempts to defend the indefensible. Two media examples provide good examples of the right and wrong way to handle a crisis.

Oprah Winfrey is an industry unto herself. Her television show, magazine, production company, and numerous philanthropic endeavors are so closely associated with the woman that it's hard to know where the person stops and the company begins. Winfrey is an icon, meaning she occupies a unique position in the culture's collective mind. In 1996, she started the Oprah Book Club. Her influence is so pervasive that being selected by her club can turn even an obscure book into a bestseller.

In 2005, Winfrey chose James Frey's "memoir" *A Million Little Pieces,* a supposedly true story of the author's journey into alcoholism, drug addiction, and crime. Based on Winfrey's emotional testimonial, the book outsold all others, with the exception of the Harry Potter series. When many of Frey's claims were questioned, Winfrey at first defended the author. But when the charges became more believable than the author, Winfrey realized that her credibility was at stake. The author was brought on the Oprah Winfrey Show four months after being selected for her book club, where the queen of compassion grilled Frey like a cheap hamburger. Not only did she get the author to admit he lied, but she also brought the publisher on the show to explain why the book was listed as nonfiction.

Winfrey understands that her success is built on trust. The next example illustrates what happens when a company loses sight of its brand promise.

It could be argued that journalism changed in the United States with the Vietnam War and the resignation of Richard Nixon. Although Walter Cronkite was voted the most trusted person in America, a generation of journalists saw Woodward and Bernstein as their role models. Bringing down a government or stopping a war seemed attainable goals for a new generation of activist reporters. The notion of impartial observer status became a quaint anachronism for the most ambitious of them.

Dan Rather certainly fit the bill of ambitious journalist. Risking his life to get stories in the middle of a hurricane or war-torn Vietnam and Afghanistan, Rather rose quickly at CBS. He also displayed a lack of respect for authority figures than endeared him to many of the Baby Boom generation. Rather took the premiere position in broadcast journalism in 1981, replacing iconic Cronkite. Rather held the position for 24 years, but during his tenure, CBS fell from number one to number three among network news shows amid an overall precipitous drop in viewership. At 72, Rather seemed to be hanging on at the twi-light of a very distinguished career. But apparently he still had enough fire in his belly to take on a sitting president.

On September 8, 2004, Rather broadcast on *60 Minutes II* that he had documents in his possession from President George W. Bush's National Guard commander. The documents were copies, but Rather assured the nation that they were legit. Within hours, bloggers showed that the documents from 1972 looked suspiciously like they had been created using Microsoft Word. Further investigation showed that a Democratic loyalist had supplied the documents, and an interview with the late commander's secretary confirmed that she had not typed the letters. CBS's own expert refused to certify the letters' authentic-ity, prompting producers to find another expert.

Rather's reaction to the tempest he created was the opposite of Winfrey's. At first he continued to insist that the documents were au-thentic, contending that anyone who said differently was partisan. He refused to concede that he or his producer had done anything wrong and seemed to resent the implications. In a final bizarre twist, he fi-nally acknowledged that the documents might be fakes, but the story was still accurate.

As a former journalist, it's hard to understand how someone of Rather's credentials could put on air a story based on a poorly verified document and then fail to mention that it came from a political oper-ative. As bad as this was for CBS news, the ensuing imbroglio that re-sulted in the dismissal of four staff members and Rather's early retirement was a PR nightmare. A panel inquiry was finally imple-mented and the publicly released report made the entire organization look unprofessional and highly biased, a contention they had been fighting for years. Ironically, the affair became known as Rathergate.

When PR is viewed as a strategic part of the marketing depart-ment, it can help keep the company aligned with its core principles. Oprah Winfrey and Tylenol both rebounded stronger than ever be-cause their response came across as sincere and their actions supported their public statements. However, when the response to a crisis appears to be only PR, the damage is magnified. The PR efforts for Dan Rather and the *Exxon Valdez* both came across as PR efforts, insincere and condescending. Rather failed to understand what Winfrey grasped immediately: Your audience has to trust you. Although Rather certainly seemed to believe the report, he failed to understand that the perception of honesty and fairness outweighs getting the story.

Ultimately, PR is about creating and maintaining the brand promise between the company and the public. To do this effectively, PR must be able to influence internal decision making and external perception.

Trust the Brand

The brand is the key to successful customer habituation. For customers to automate a purchase or use decision, they must trust the brand. A lack of trust will keep a decision under the control of the executive mind. People might vary widely in their initial willingness to trust, but when a trust is violated, the vast majority will never fully trust the violator again. Conversely, when trust is established, a customer will want to maintain the relationship, resisting overtures by competing brands. Loyalty comes from trust.

A report from the Radiological Society of North America reveals that well-known brands activate positive emotional responses in our brains. These strong activations occur regardless of product category—our brains are conditioned by the brand, not the product. The areas affected are associated with self-identification and rewards.

Customers are not loyal to a brand as they are loyal to a friend or a spouse. Customers do not feel that they are betraying a company by buying a competing brand or shopping at a competitor's store unless they actually have a friendship with specific people at a company. Customers are loyal to trusted brands because these products simplify their choices. Buying a competing brand means having to engage the executive mind.

To build trust, a company must understand what its brand promises. The brand promise is the deal, the contract between a customer and a company—but it's an unwritten contract. By consistently delivering on its brand promise, a company can facilitate the transference of a decision from the executive mind to the habitual mind. Brands that lack a clear promise do not create differentiation and fail to gain a stronghold as part of customers' habitual repertoire.

This shows why the role of the brand in habitual behavior cannot be overstated. The brand is the lynchpin in a customer's ability to automate a decision. Companies would do well to continuously market their brand identity internally as well as externally. It is not enough for the brand manager to understand a brand's vision and strategy because decisions made by other managers, marketers, and executives can influence the perception of the brand.

Decisions that impact the brand can come from anywhere, including finance and legal departments. Blockbuster lost $57 million the first quarter after canceling its hated late fees, but the policy was a political nightmare for the company and customers were flocking to Netflix, which doesn't charge late fees. Wireless carriers are addicted to punitive fees charged to customers who go over their monthly minutes or leave before contract expirations. I have participated in countless discussions with wireless executives defending these policies. From a finance perspective, these decisions seem easy—they generate billions in profits. But the cost is measured in defection rates that cost these same companies billions. Fred Reicheld, a Bain Fellow and founder of Bain's Loyalty practice, refers to the tactics as creating bad profits.

In relationship businesses, violating a trust is taken personally. When my stockbroker recommended an investment product that I knew would pay him a large commission but was in disfavor with financial planners, it was only a matter of time before I left him. The experience left me feeling angry and betrayed. If I couldn't trust him, I would have to evaluate every decision and recommendation he made, so why pay him in the first place?

Brands can also suffer when changes are made to products, services, pricing, or distribution channels. Cost-saving decisions that make sense on a spreadsheet can prove disastrous if they violate the customer's perception of the brand promise. Many companies who have moved customer service offshore have experienced pronounced declines in their ability to deliver acceptable levels of customer service. Similarly, substituting inexpensive components and reducing service levels can break the brand promise.

The brand comes to represent the sum total of a customer's experience with a product or a company. Sometimes one violation of the brand promise is all it takes, as Nielsen's Srivatsa points out with baby products that cause a rash. However, habits are persistent, developing their own inertia. When companies reduce the quality of a product or service, we don't typically see a mass defection. A large majority of customers continue to buy the product pretty much the same way they always have. Losses are usually less than 5% above normal attrition. Anything greater would be a clear indicator that the change was an error, forcing the company to backtrack and fix it.

Our customers' habitual behavior can mask our mistakes, giving the incorrect impression that cost-cutting decisions that impacted quality were justified. But whether you are a beer maker that found a way to shorten the brewing process or a retail outlet that started charging a restocking fee for returns, you might end up breaking your brand's promise and cause long-term declines in growth and profitability.

The Physical Brand

A key component to a brand's ability to help customers automate purchase and use is its physical attributes. The American Marketing Association's definition of brand includes a name, term, design, or symbol that distinguishes products and services from competitive offerings.

Habits are created through repetition of behavior under stable conditions or contexts. Any stimuli associated with the context can become a cue that will trigger the behavior. The power of brands is that they can become the cue or the part of habitual behavior activated by a cue.

Intel faced an incredibly challenging marketing problem: how to leverage its favorable brand image when its main product was invisible to the customers who bought it. The Intel Inside campaign was effective because it combined a highly visible advertising blitz with the company's logo on the outside of the computer. Compaq, the PC market leader at the time, declined to participate, recognizing that Intel Inside would diminish the value of its brand. However, the campaign was so successful that Compaq eventually capitulated because customers were checking to make sure Intel was the processor inside the PCs they bought.

Every aspect of the product can become a cue, especially logos, brand marks, brand names, and packaging. The Intel chime was an integral part of its successful elevation to customer awareness. When customers are shopping on autopilot, they rely on the familiarity of the physical appearance of a product, including packaging and branding, to automate their behavior. The shape of the traditional Coke bottle is an integral part of numerous marketing campaigns. Similarly, the physical appearances of stores, restaurants, and web sites can serve as cues to activate a wide range of behaviors.

Any change in appearance represents a potential risk of removing the stimulus that serves as the cue. I experienced this personally not long ago when I walked right by the box of Italian seasonings I was looking for. In a move to update the look, the manufacturer had radically changed the appearance of the box, including its distinctive color. Because I was in automatic mode, the new box was essentially invisible. I was able to find it only because it was on my list and the grocer had put the box in the exact same position on the store shelf.

The brand can also be part of the habitual response to other cues that activate behavior. Going to a bar might activate a habit of ordering a draft beer. Your normal brand isn't available on tap, but you spy your favorite European brand on one of the tap handles. Although it's more expensive, the decision to splurge is almost automatic. Understanding the customer's context for a purchase is critical to understanding the heuristic they will use.

Another example from Srivatsa in the pharmaceutical field illustrates this point. "Shoppers may buy generic drugs for themselves but will buy the name brand for their loved ones. Intellectually, they know they are the same, but emotionally, they want to feel they are sparing no expense for their child or spouse." The context determines which heuristic will be used.

The brand is both the physical representation of a product or company's identity and the sum total experience customers have with the product or company. Both definitions are essential to habit formation. It is critical to observe customers and potential customers to understand how they interact with the brand.

Although any change to a product can impact brand perception, I cover pricing and distribution channels separately because their impact on habit formation is profound.

Marketing Research

Marketing as a discipline is progressively becoming more scientific through advances in research techniques. From data mining to behavioral tracking, recent advances in acquiring and analyzing data provide an increasing level of confidence for managers to make decisions—in theory. Yet with all this information at their fingertips, executives and managers seem to be making pretty much the same mistakes that they've always made. The hits seem to come from inspiration or vision, and myriad failures seem to have been logical after looking at the data.

At the heart of this dilemma is the fact that most market research examines the executive mind while the habitual mind is driving the bus. The historical knowledge that managers have relied upon is therefore compromised because it is based on the flawed assumption that our customers know why they do what they do. This cannot be overemphasized because so much of what we think we know is based on this flawed assumption. This is why the new product introduction failure rate remains unchanged and customers continue to leave, regardless of their satisfaction levels.

Managers might want to believe the marketing research, but their gut tells them not to rely too heavily on the data. Market researchers, in turn, feel frustrated that the value of their contribution is not recognized. What is needed is an understanding of what the data is actually measuring, whether it is information captured from the executive or habitual minds.

I had the privilege of studying under Naresh Malhotra Ph.D., Regent's Professor of Marketing at Georgia Institute of Technology. Recognized as one of the most prolific researchers in the world, Dr. Malhotra imbued in me a strong respect for the integrity of the data from collection to analysis to conclusion. His *Marketing Research* textbook is considered one of the best on the subject and is used on college campuses across the country. Under his tutelage, I learned how to choose a research methodology to apply to specific marketing questions. After the data was collected, I was trained to apply a wide range of rigorous single and multivariate statistical analyses from simple regression to causal modeling. Dr. Malhotra is a stickler for statistical integrity, making sure every step of research is subject to internal and external tests of validation.

Combining this training with my experience teaching statistics for five years, I became a strong advocate of marketing research, of arming managers with knowledge, not just information. My attitude could be summed up as "The more quantitative, the better." In that light, I looked down on most qualitative research as lacking in rigor, reliability, and statistical validity.

Based on the discoveries outlined in Chapter 2, my attitude toward market research has undergone a profound modification. Market researchers have long divided studies into two categories: qualitative and quantitative. Qualitative methods usually employ small samples with open-ended formats such as focus groups and in-depth interviewing. Quantitative research covers a wide spectrum of techniques, from simple cross tabs to advanced mathematical modeling. Researchers often view qualitative and quantitative research as complimentary, with the former providing insights that can be examined with the latter. But both qualitative and quantitative research have the same Achilles' heel: They often fail to capture the unconscious habits and scripts that are actually guiding customer behavior.

Yet great data is being collected and analyzed with powerful statistical tools that can give managers tremendous insights. How can managers know what data is reliable and what needs to be used with caution?

The primary difference is whether the data is collected based on the habitual mind (actual behavior or in-depth techniques) or the executive mind (surveys, questionnaires, focus groups). When I explained this difference to Alan Weber, president of Kansas City database consulting company Marketing Analytics Group, he immediately made the connection. "What you are saying is that instead of looking at the database as a record of transactions, it's actually a record of customer behavior." Companies are sitting on vast sums of information—in effect, a behavioral database.

Myriad techniques exist for extracting value from this data. Data mining is a brute-force method of examining purchases and looking for nontrivial connections that are not apparent to traditional statistical analysis. However, we can use a variety of statistical methods to extract a better understanding of what customers are doing and, more important, what they will do in the future. Numerous research studies indicate that current customers often telegraph future intentions through changes in purchase patterns. Does your organization know the behavioral indicators of soon-to-be defecting customers?

A company's electronic presence also provides enormous data that it can analyze and act upon. However, few companies integrate their online presence with their customer databases other than in order processing.

Getting qualitative data from the habitual mind requires somewhat of an indirect approach. As explained previously, metaphors can be a highly effective tool in uncovering the influence of the habitual mind. The difficulty in this approach is that it is time consuming, takes a trained interviewer, and does not lend itself to statistical validation. However, the insights gleaned from this type of research can be invaluable to product managers, marketers, and product designers.

Quantitative methods, such as conjoint analysis, capture unconscious influences. In this statistical procedure, subjects rank order cards that list a variety of product attributes, such as brand name, price, and features. Because respondents are presented with more variables than the executive mind can accommodate, the unconscious scripts of the habitual mind are accessed.

Both Donald Norman and Harry West emphasize the importance for designers to observe actual customers in real-life situations. Observation is equally important in market research. Capturing this information and developing a method of communicating resulting insights is critical for how you approach the marketplace. Executives and managers who do not supplement research reports with actual visits to where their customers work, shop, and live will never fully understand what the research has to tell them.

Market intelligence companies are advancing behavioral research with technology that tracks customers as they move through stores and view web sites. This type of information can help us understand the underlying habitual patterns of our customers' lives, but this information alone will not uncover the subtle emotional and social influences that invisibly guide behavior.

The next decade will undoubtedly reveal far more about the implications of the brain's multiple minds. This opens up tremendous opportunities for companies to rethink and reposition their marketing to better align with how customers are actually interacting with their brands.

Part III

Treat Your Customers Like Dogs

7

Of Google and Cigarettes

"We don't sell Tic Tacs; we sell cigarettes. And they're cool, and available ... and addictive. The job is almost done for you."

BR in *Thank You for Smoking*

Cigarettes will kill you. They will give you cancer. They will give you emphysema. They make your breath stink. When you smoke, little lines become etched around your mouth. You can know and believe all this, but if you are addicted to cigarettes, it doesn't matter. Consciously, you are convinced that cigarettes are a threat to your life, but your unconscious keeps reaching for the pack in your pocket or purse.

Within a year of surgery, almost half of lung cancer patients return to smoking. The enormity of that statistic vividly illustrates the power of the habitual mind. Part of your lung is being removed because you are sucking on poison, but neural circuits in the limbic region of your brain are still dying for a smoke. The addictive process provides a unique view into the workings of habits.

Nicotine is the addictive component in cigarettes; it is also remarkably toxic. It is the tobacco plant's defense mechanism against insects. Drop for drop, nicotine is more poisonous than strychnine or rattlesnake venom. But in the human brain, nicotine triggers the release of dopamine, the neurotransmitter associated with pleasure and reward in the limbic system—the same circuit cocaine affects. Nicotine is a stimulant, yet it paradoxically triggers feelings of both stimulation and relaxation, usually depending on the mental and physical state of the user.

For several years, I was a counselor and program director in alcohol and drug treatment centers. As hard as it was to get clients off cocaine, alcohol, and meth, cigarettes were even harder. I think the twin effects of physical stimulation and emotional calming make cigarette addiction so intractable. If a smoker is feeling anxious, that anxiety triggers the need for a cigarette to calm down. If the same person is feeling tired, he knows a cigarette will give him a boost. Cigarettes also serve as an appetite suppressant, making them popular with women. And because cigarettes are legal, smokers have developed hundreds of cues in their everyday environment that trigger lighting up.

Knowing how the habitual brain is responsible for most of our behavior helps us understand the apparently insane behavior of the addict. Responding to cues both in the environment and inside their bodies, addicts are reacting to powerful habits that are being triggered entirely outside of conscious awareness. The executive mind might be able to halt this process for a while, but at significant psychic cost. When the person gets tired or distracted, the habit comes back with a vengeance. In fact, the addicted mind conscripts the executive mind, which actively denies the influence of the drug.

Addiction is the extreme of habit formation. The feedback mechanism becomes broken, causing the afflicted to participate in self-harming behavior. Drugs such as nicotine, cocaine, and alcohol disrupt the normal habit-forming process by interfering with neurotransmitters and receptors. But this pernicious disease process shows us what we miss most of the time—that our unconscious habits control us. When this system functions properly, these same neurotransmitters and receptors train the brain to respond to the environment efficiently and effectively, without executive intervention. Although not as compulsive as an addiction, habitual behavior has a similar kind of force, which brings us to Google.

Mark Hutcheson—my researcher, project manager, personal day planner, and long-time friend—told me about this great new search engine in late 1998 or early 1999, shortly after Google's first public, but still beta, release. I was working for a small research and consulting company, and the Internet had become a tremendous resource, making my trips to the library much less frequent. When I was doing my graduate work in the early 1990s, I started out using Archie to search the fledgling World Wide Web and progressed through a series of search engines, including Excite, Lycos, and AltaVista after leaving school. By 1999, I was using various search engines, one for business articles, another for science information, and another for items such as hotels and restaurants. When I started using Google, it quickly became my go-to search engine.

Google had the uncanny ability to return exactly what I was looking for as the first or second link, and it delivered the results with amazing speed. Along with the hundreds of millions who followed, I quickly became hooked on the algorithm created by Larry Page and Sergey Brin that ran on networked PCs instead of big mainframe computers. At first, I was pleasantly surprised by how well Google worked, but pretty soon I stopped thinking about Google at all. I no longer chose to use Google—I used it completely out of habit.

The thesis of this book is that marketplace success inevitably comes from this process. Google serves as an excellent example because it shows how the executive mind is initially involved in choice but rapidly hands off a task that has been repeatedly solved. Initially, I consciously decided to use Google based on a recommendation from a trusted source. The home page did not win me over, but the accuracy and speed of results were great. The combination of recommendation and personal experience caused me to develop a conscious preference, but the reliability of Google's performance rapidly transferred this conscious choice into an unconscious habit.

The neural circuitry of my brain went through a physiological change. Associations were being made surrounding the context of a task and cues in the environment. For example, by creating a Google bookmark, I made it easier to automate its selection. The Google taskbar makes habit formation even more automatic. I progressively expanded my Google habit to my Treo phones and other Internet devices.

Google developed a brilliant business model to go with its habitual service—charging advertisers access to the millions of eyeballs continuously reviewing Google search results. In less than ten years, the company started by two Ph.D. students in a dorm room had a market capitalization more than 14 times that of GM simply by becoming our habitual choice for a routine activity.

8

Behavioral Training

In Part I, the implications of the remarkable discovery that our unconscious minds control most our behavior. Part II briefly updated basic marketing concepts based on this insight. But simply knowing that our customer's unconscious mind is influencing behavior isn't very helpful. This last section, introduced by "Of Google and Cigarettes," provides a blueprint for working with our customer's habitual and executive minds to become the customers' habit. The short version is simple: Treat your customers like dogs.

Although this sounds particularly counterintuitive, this idea is based on one of the most heavily researched and validated areas in psychology. We don't have established marketing rules to guide us, but we do have a sound, well-researched platform available to help: behavioral training. Although this discipline comes from the world of behavioral biology and animal training, it has been applied to a wide set of human applications, including working with autistic children and amateur and professional athletes.

Many people object to behavioral conditioning because they misunderstand the habit formation process. They believe that the reinforcer is essentially buying behavior and that it must be maintained if the behavior is to persist. The goal of habit formation is to automate behavior so it doesn't need to be externally reinforced.

The habitual mind is nonverbal, so it doesn't learn by reading or listening to an explanation. It learns unconsciously through associating an action with an outcome. This is the system we must influence.

This idea is foreign to most of our marketing thought, which focuses on either conscious appeals to action or indirect appeals to emotion.

Anyone taking psychology courses after 1965 likely encountered behaviorism and its most famous advocate, B. F. Skinner. Although behaviorism made numerous advances in our understanding of animal and human behavior, it rejected what was going on inside the black box of the conscious mind. If behaviorists couldn't observe it, it didn't matter. Skinner, an atheist, further alienated the general public with his books *Walden Two* and *Beyond Freedom and Dignity*, in which he questioned the existence of free will. However, early behaviorists were on to something very important.

In the first section of the book, we saw how scientists can now peer inside the black box using fMRI, PET scans, and other advanced techniques. This gives us a much more balanced view of both executive and habitual mind functioning. We can now combine Skinner's insights with advances in cognitive psychology to radically rethink our approach to customers and the marketplace without denying God's existence or man's free will.

We now know that the executive mind is real and that places in our minds house our sense of identity and morality. We understand that our mirror neurons connect us intimately to our fellow man in ways Skinner could never have imagined. We understand how emotions help us better interact with the world and make decisions. But we also know that habits are formed by the repetition of behaviors, actions real people perform in real situations to solve problems.

Therefore, companies must create programs oriented around behavioral outcomes instead of attitudes and beliefs. This means focusing on not just the transaction, but on every behavior leading up to and after the transaction. This requires marketers, managers, executives, product designers, retail outlets, and service companies to radically rethink their approach to the marketplace.

The rules for training the habitual mind are as real as those governing the movements of the planets. Although university researchers have examined these rules extensively, we see them implemented most successfully in the world of training. Whether with animal trainers working with dolphins or an instructor working with a novice golfer, the results from using these techniques are effective and reliable.

Behavioral training is effective because it works with the way the habitual mind learns. The habitual brain learns the same way a dog learns. The power of the executive brain is its ability to think abstractly about the world, but the power of the habitual brain is its ability to interact with the world on its own terms.

"Training customers" sounds manipulative and condescending, but it's not. "Training customers" means working with, not against, their habitual minds. Your customers must be trained on how to get to your store, where to look for your services, and how to navigate your web site. If they're not trained, they need to use their executive mind, which is inefficient and frustrating.

An obvious byproduct of this line of thinking is the need to make your products, services, and customer interfaces as intuitive as possible. Habits are formed much faster and more reliably with simple, elegant designs and interfaces.

Customers are being trained all the time, but haphazardly by you, the environment, and your competitors. Training customers to use your products and services with minimal effort requires reinforcing specific behaviors in a timely fashion. Let's look at how behavioral training works.

Karen Pryor Shapes a Generation of Trainers

Karen Pryor, internationally recognized behavioral biologist, author, and expert trainer, has been positively reinforcing animals since she became the lead dolphin trainer for Hawaii's Sea Life Park in 1963. She talked with me about training with reinforcement and how to apply these principles to humans.

"Any behavior that is occurring can be reinforced," Pryor explained to me from her home in Massachusetts. It's important to remember that behavior must occur before it can be reinforced. "If you call a puppy and it comes to you, and then you give it a pat or a treat, it will start coming to you reliably when you call it. But if the puppy doesn't come, you can't reinforce the behavior." This is where positive reinforcement is different from traditional training. Coercion isn't used; the trainer waits until a behavior happens and then reinforces it.

We can reinforce any behavior, no matter how sporadically it occurs, Pryor explains. "We call this shaping." A dolphin doesn't jump through a ring on command all at once, but only after a series of intermediate behaviors have been shaped through progressive reinforcement.

Customers are constantly having their behaviors shaped, often abusively. For example, calling in to customer service, we are prompted to push 1 for English, wait to hear what our choices are from a menu of indeterminate length, push more buttons, and enter account numbers to accomplish tasks as divergent as questioning a bill to ordering products.

I have used Pryor's classic book *Don't Shoot the Dogs* as a guidebook for training my three Border collies, and I commented that I often feel incompetent. "None of us are great trainers," she assured me. "Behavioral training is simple, but it is not easy."

With that in mind, let's break down behavioral training into its constituent parts and then look at how to put it all together to create customers who use our products and services without a thought. The areas we cover are reinforcement and punishment, timing, nonverbal reinforcement, shaping, and conditioned reinforcement.

Calling for Reinforcements

The habitual mind learns through feedback such as in stimulus-response (classical conditioning) or in modification of voluntary behavior (operant conditioning). Reinforcement is feedback that occurs close to a behavior that makes that behavior more likely to occur in the future. But moving beyond Psych 101, this obvious concept is devilishly tricky to work with.

By definition, anything that increases the likelihood that a behavior will occur in the future is a reinforcer. Although we understand this as common sense, we screw up all the time. Most parents are familiar with inadvertently reinforcing an unwanted behavior, such as giving a whining child candy or a toy to be quiet. Oops, we just trained our child to whine. Companies do this as well. A customer leaves us, and we offer her a much better deal to get her back. Oops, we just trained our customer to leave us.

Reinforcers come in two flavors, positive and negative. It's important to remember that both make a behavior more likely to occur. A negative reinforcer is not a punishment—but more on that later.

A positive reinforcer is anything that a customer wants. For the sake of simplicity, let's call a positive reinforcer a cookie. Cookies come in different sizes and different flavors. Not everybody likes the same flavor of cookie, so to actually reinforce a behavior, the cookie has to be in a flavor the customer likes. A teacher who heaps praise on a shy student thinks he's giving a cookie but is instead punishing her behavior.

In general, cookies serve as feedback mechanisms and are not simply rewards. Pryor explains that trainers used to underfeed animals so they would work harder for food, but this is not only unnecessary, but also counterproductive. However, the more demanding the behavior, the bigger the cookie needed.

A negative reinforcer is something the customer doesn't like that is removed when a behavior is performed. For the sake of simplicity, let's call negative reinforcers buzzers. My life seems controlled by buzzers. My alarm clock buzzes until I get up to turn it off. The timer on the washer buzzes until I move the laundry to the dryer. The microwave beeps until I open its door. My car buzzes until I put on my seat belt. A buzzer can also be a bored look on a colleague's face as you drone on in a meeting. If his facial expression relaxes when you stop talking, you have just been negatively reinforced.

Let's look at a quick example to show how tricky reinforcers can be. A ringing phone is a buzzer. When you pick up the phone, the irritating sound stops—a classic example of negative reinforcement. But digital technology enables us to put ringers on our mobile phones that are not aversive, such as a short clip of a favorite song or the sound of a clucking chicken. People with customized ring tones are slower answering their cell phones than are people with preset ringers—unless that customized ring tone is embarrassing in a given surrounding. One of my wife's patients, a police officer, had the *Cops* theme song "Bad Boys" as her ring tone. This was cute until the day she forgot to silence her phone while in court. In other words, a cookie can become a buzzer, depending on the context of a situation.

A punishment is something that makes a behavior less likely to occur. As with reinforcement, a punishment can be the introduction of something unpleasant, such as a spanking, or removal of something enjoyable, such as grabbing a toy away from a child who is making too much noise. The problem with punishments is that they tell you what not to do without guiding what you should do. You can do anything in a million wrong ways. At best, punishment eliminates only one of them.

A classic illustration is attempting to shape a mouse's behavior to go to a particular corner of a cage. One approach is to put an electric grid in the floor of the cage. The mouse receives shocks when it moves anywhere in the cage but the desired corner. The mouse will need to discover a lot of places not to go before it eventually stumbles on the right area where it will not be punished. The mouse is likely to become neurotic from the experience. It's much easier and faster to allow the mouse to wander about the cage unmolested and simply give it a piece of chocolate (preferably Belgian) when it goes to the designated corner.

Companies routinely punish the behavior they should encourage. From an example we used earlier, cell phone companies charge more per minute after customers exceed the number of minutes in their plan. Instead of encouraging customers to use their cell phones, carriers discourage them. Similarly, airlines that put in narrower seats to add another row are punishing flyers whose butts aren't getting smaller.

What Pryor has discovered, along with thousands of other researchers and trainers, is that giving cookies is the best way to shape behavior. By giving cookies, we are communicating very clearly, "That's it!" She contrasts positive reinforcement with old-school reward and punishment, terms she does not use in her training methodology.

"Let's say you're trying to get a dog to sit. With positive reinforcement, you put a treat in front of his nose, raise it up, and move it forward. The dog's natural response is to put his rump on the floor. If you say 'sit' as he does this and give him a treat at the same time, he will quickly learn to associate 'sit' with an action that gets him a treat."

Pryor points out that in correction-based training, the cues can become confusing. "Novice trainers will reward a dog for sitting for several trials, but then think he should 'get it.' When the dog doesn't sit on cue, the novice jerks on the leash. 'Sit' has become a poison cue, one that might get a reward or a punishment." Companies do this when they send sales pitches stuffed with a bill or try to sell you something when you call customer service with a complaint. The cue takes on multiple meanings, making the customer anxious.

Think through your organization's relationship with its customers. Examine every interface between the firm and the customer for reinforcers and punishments. Are you reinforcing the behaviors you want? Are you punishing the behaviors you don't want? Have poison cues slipped into your communications? Is your customer service an oxymoron?

Companies routinely create these problems by trying to save money or make more money. In his book *Gotcha Capitalism*, Bob Sullivan lists some of the most egregious offenders who profit through deceptive practices such as burying cost details in text so small he calls it "mouseprint." Companies are undoubtedly making billions annually through such practices, but they engender customer backlash by disrupting habitual behavior.

A Matter of Timing

The timing of reinforcements is essential to the training process. Remember that the habitual mind is learning via this feedback mechanism. The closer the reinforcement is to the behavior, the faster the association will be made, and the quicker the neural circuits will form. A computer mouse is exceptionally intuitive to learn because it responds instantly to the movement of our hand. A rebate that you need to mail in is far less reinforcing than a sticker on the package that you can redeem at the register. "We have a naïve belief in the power of words to cover up our lapses in timing," Pryor explains.

When we reinforce behavior too quickly, we train the subject to not complete the behavior. Returning to the example of teaching a puppy to come, let's say that you call the puppy and he starts running toward you. You get excited and say "Good boy" before he gets all the way to you. The puppy sits down three feet away from you.

Salespeople routinely reinforce prematurely. For example, in trying to win a large contract, a salesperson might take potential clients to special events, nice restaurants, and golf outings. The client is reinforced for not purchasing. As soon as the purchase is decided, the nice things go away, turning the purchase into a punishment.

We must also remember that the cookie needs to come after the behavior. We are often tempted to show the reward to encourage behavior. This is bribery. Our goal is to establish habits, and bribery works with the executive, not the habitual, mind.

However, our biggest problem is delayed reinforcement. Our paychecks are a good example, often coming so far after the behavior being reinforced that little connection exists between what we are doing and what we are getting paid for. Worse, the annual review process seeks to somehow improve our performance by waiting a year to tell us what we are doing wrong or right.

Most loyalty programs introduce long delays between behavior and cookie. My primary airline requires 25,000 miles to earn a domestic ticket, 50,000 miles if I want to use points for international travel. The insurance industry faces the daunting task of selling a product whose reinforcer might not come for years, if ever. Companies that have long delays between behavior and cookie need to create intermediary reinforcement, a type of cue that signals you are on the right track. Allstate has a good driver policy that reinforces safe driving. By rebating money, the company creates an annual cookie for its best customers.

Conditioned Reinforcers to the Rescue

Pryor is a strong advocate of clicker training, in which a click is paired with a reinforcer multiple times until the click becomes a conditioned reinforcer. If a dog hears a click just before getting a cookie, it associates the click with the cookie. The habitual mind is not learning simply how to get food, but how to get along in the environment. Conditioned reinforcers are just another way of forming shortcuts, making them useful for building habits.

For example, because it can take a long time to earn a trip with frequent flyer miles, airlines could develop a conditioned reinforcer. Imagine receiving an auditory or visual cue at the airport kiosk at check-in. A small chime or visual representation could signal travelers that the trip they are taking is getting them close to a free trip or merchandise. This immediate feedback would strongly reinforce my airline choice. The future trip is a reward that lives only in the executive mind; the click would become a reinforcer for the habitual mind.

Pryor is adamant that using positive reinforcement is the best way to work with people, dogs, horses, and even fish. "Whether you're working with animals or people, positive reinforcement is far more humane and respectful than any of the alternatives, such as punishment or coercion. It's also far more effective."

I think a profound error for us as managers, parents, and marketers is not appreciating which mind we are working with. In raising children, parents want to instill strong morals and ethics. They want their children to be honest, thoughtful, hard working, and conscientious. But they yell at them for not keeping their rooms clean and not washing the dishes. In the minds of parents (myself definitely included), confusion exists between bad behavior (lying, stealing, bullying) and poor training (not keeping a room clean, failing to study for a test). Although picking up your clothes in not an ethical issue, we make it so by treating our children's failure in this area as a sign they're being bad. A lack of proper training is a failure of habit, not of morals.

The same concept is muddled in our heads when we describe customer loyalty. The word *loyal* carries an exceptional amount of baggage. If you are a disloyal spouse or a disloyal soldier, you have violated the sacred cannons of important societal institutions. Should we really think that our customers owe us this kind of loyalty? If your customers aren't loyal, it means that they have not been properly trained, not that they have violated a code of conduct.

Customers are using your product, service, store, web site, or search engine to solve their problems. Training them means you are helping them become more efficient in getting their tasks done by using your company. As I described the idea behind this book to Pryor, she laughed and said, "You're right. The reinforcer is not having to think about it. I don't know the brand of detergent I buy; I just know it's the one in the blue bottle."

Instead of being manipulative, using behavioral conditioning with reinforcers and conditioned reinforcers lets people know exactly what is expected of them. It also puts them in control of the situation. Many of us have experienced the frustration of dealing with insurance companies that seem to arbitrarily disallow services we think our policy should cover. As companies become more global, they create layers of insulation between themselves and their customers, inhibiting the two-way feedback mechanisms that can ensure long-term, profitable relationships.

Talking to the Habitual Mind

The habitual mind does not understand language, so reinforcers need to be nonverbal. "That part of our brain is nonverbal," Pryor confirms. "An abstract gesture is better than words." Pryor is involved with a company, TAGteach, which applies clicker-training techniques to a wide variety of teaching and coaching tasks. TAG is an acronym for Teaching with Acoustical Guidance. A TAG is an audible cookie that lets a student know they are doing the right thing. "By using an audio cue, students don't have to process time-consuming language analysis in the middle of a complex behavior."

Her comment brought to mind the first trainer my daughter went to for horse-riding lessons. Shouts of "grab mane," "sit up," "get your heels down," and "No! No! No!" echoed across the ring. Although the trainer knew her stuff, her reliance on words engaged my daughter's executive mind for habitual mind responsibilities. I could never figure out how my 12-year-old daughter was supposed to process that kind of information while guiding a 1,500-pound horse over a 3-foot jump.

The TAG method relies on a relatively new approach in behavioral training. The TAG point is established for a specific behavior, and students get an audible cookie when they get to the TAG point. Mistakes are ignored. The only message the students get comes when they execute the behavior properly. Students are making remarkable progress using these techniques, often mastering complex movement in minutes instead of taking weeks using verbal explanations.

This type of training shapes complex behavior by breaking it down into constituent parts. We can break down a purchase process similar to how we can break down a golf swing. Creating purchase habits typically requires customers to go through multiple steps. The idea of training a customer to be able to automate this process requires a company to look at how it can simplify things for the customer and reinforce each step as it occurs.

For example, ideally, you want your products and services to enjoy a good merchandising position, making it easier for your customer to find them. However, these placements come at a significant cost, and only a handful of brands can take these coveted positions. If a brand is hard to find, a store is hard to get to, or a web site is hard to remember, marketers must develop a training mechanism to shape the customer's behavior.

Armed with the basics of how to shape behaviors, the last section of the book provides a blueprint of how to become your customer's habit.

9

Behavioral Marketing[1]: Becoming Your Customer's Habit

Increasing competitive intensity seems to be one of the few constants in today's business environment. Customers are inundated with thousands of brands, many more thousands of advertising messages a day, and an ever-changing landscape of brick-and-mortar and electronic distribution channels. Creating a sustainable competitive advantage in this environment is increasingly difficult because everybody is fighting for the same piece of real estate—a position in the executive mind of customers. But as we have seen throughout this book, they are fighting the wrong fight on the wrong battlefield.

The real fight for customers is taking place in their unconscious, habitual minds. I call this process behavioral marketing, which seeks to make purchase and repurchase so automatic that customers do not have to think. To win this battle, companies need to approach the process of winning and keeping customers from a behavioral perspective. Although attitudes, emotions, and beliefs play a role in purchase and usage, their impact is limited to early stages of habit formation.

Creating a universal process for customer habituation across industries is impossible, but several components of habit formation can serve as a blueprint. Let's break this into two parts: habit formation and habit maintenance.

[1] *Behavioral marketing* has been used narrowly as a term to describe tracking behavior on web sites, but that function is more commonly referred to as behavioral targeting. In this book, *behavioral marketing* refers to a broad range of marketing activities designed to elicit specific behaviors leading to habit formation.

Discovery

To form a habit, customers must repeat three sets of behaviors: discovery, purchase, and use.

Discovery involves all the steps that a noncustomer goes through before making a purchase. How do customers find out about products in a given category? Does advertising affect them? If so, which media? Do they go to web sites? If so, which ones? Do they rely on friends or trusted sources? Do customers need to see or touch the product to buy it?

Properly positioning a brand into this discovery process is an important first step. Working with prospective customers' existing search habits is a much more efficient use of advertising dollars. Also, matching the target market's method of discovery helps the category neurons in the PFC position the brand appropriately. Companies often work against the mental habits of the unconscious mind and need to ratchet up the volume just to get noticed.

For example, in business-to-business (B2B) sales, small to medium-sized companies often rely on a trusted influencer such as a consultant or value-add reseller. Attempting to bypass this influencer with ads or sales calls will not be effective. You must sell the influencer before you have a chance with the decision maker.

Similarly, it is important to understand how different segments explore information. Although Walt Mossberg of the *Wall Street Journal* might heavily influence people over the age of 40, younger demographics might look for information on the same product by going to the irreverent video podcasts of Kevin Rose and Alex Albrecht of DiggNation.

The shift in advertising to the Internet is a good example of how changing habits create new threats and opportunities. Google's business model taps into the thousands of small businesses that cannot afford traditional advertising but can instead use AdWords to reach their limited audience. But Google understands that habitual behavior is linked to reinforcement, so ads are rank-ordered on a quality score (based on click-through and relevance) and the bid price.

The Internet has also become a favored marketing vehicle for Hollywood. Setting up a web site and having fans download trailers is much cheaper than buying airtime on television. The movie trailer is its own art form, but long gone are the days when a trailer alone gets us to the theater. Movie reviews are just a click away, and producers who opt not to prescreen movies for critics are assumed to be marketing a bomb. The review megasite Metacritic.com flags movies that have not been reviewed, offering a clear warning to users to enter at their own risk.

The next component of the front end of building habits is to communicate on a salient issue that is critical to the executive mind. At the early phases of the purchase process, the brand must appeal to a key issue that customers in this segment have identified as critical to purchase. This might be an issue of perception of need, levels of quality, reliability, price, or some other variable. If the message does not resonate on a critical factor, customers probably will not notice, but, even if they do, it won't lead to habituation.

For example, if price is not a critical factor in a product category, but a company heavily promotes its price advantage, the company might get a sale. However, unless the trial usage reveals a connection on a more important issue, it will not lead to the type of repeat purchase behavior necessary for habit formation. A dry cleaner might offer a special on shirts and blouses, which causes you to try them out. But if the location is not convenient, you won't use it habitually.

Prepurchase advertising needs to spark a behavior. Karen Pryor's observation that a behavior must occur before it can be reinforced is critical for marketers to understand. During training sessions, animals and students voluntarily offer behavior looking for reinforcement. Ads should facilitate trial behavior by getting customers to look for a product in the store, and also by getting them to look for the product in the real world. An ad that could get a potential customer to say "Hey, can I look at that?" to a friend or colleague advances the purchase process all the way to trial.

Conversely, advertising can make social discourse less likely. The level of negativity in political advertising makes it difficult to actually talk politics anymore. The major political parties have crafted wedge issues that turn policy differences into moral Armageddon. Politicians should remember that voters make two judgments on a candidate—one with the executive brain and one with the emotional brain. They vote based on emotion.

If your reaction to this is "And that's what's wrong with the country," you are missing a central component of habit formation. Although emotions can be manipulated, they are central to making good decisions. If you sense that a politician is dishonest, that information is probably more important than whether you agree with his or her public stance on immigration. The problem is that negative emotions such as fear are more likely to spur you to vote than positive emotions. Although you might logically weigh the issues, the cue that gets you to the ballot box will likely bypass your executive brain altogether.

Purchase

The executive mind often drives the initial purchase, but as with voting, the habitual mind influences the decision. We can view purchase as a threshold that must be overcome. But for many products, the first purchase either leads seamlessly to the second or is the last time the consumer ever buys the product.

Creating a strategy to get customers to try a product is critical to purchase, but even more important to repurchase. As covered previously, a customer needs to visit a store multiple times to create an internal map of the environment. Until that happens, the executive mind is occupied trying to figure out where to go. Kohl's department store shows the power of behavioral marketing.

When Kohl's enters a market, the company mails valuable coupons that strongly encourage experimental shopping. But the executives at Kohl's understand that their goal is not simply to get someone to try their store. They are looking for repeat customers. So shoppers who use that coupon are mailed another. And if they use the second one, they get a third. Instead of creating a strategy in which the coupon becomes a cue to shop, Kohl's uses the coupon to reinforce behavior. It is probably not coincidental that the Wisconsin-based department store has outperformed its peers for several years.

This example shows the importance of understanding what behaviors the customer must execute and the number of times they must execute them for habit formation to occur. Companies should strive to simplify the habit formation process as much as possible. Every additional step that a company forces the customer to go through must be repeated at least three times before it becomes etched in the habitual mind.

Product goods represent a different habituation process. By understanding that customers want to automate purchases, product managers need to identify the elements under their control that will make this easy. Nielsen's Gordon points to research showing that customers who purchase a brand eight times have up to a 97% likelihood of buying the product a ninth time. He also reports that brand equity explains very little of this persistence.

This helps explain why the major brands are so dominant. It's market inertia. Customers continue to buy out of routine. When markets begin to change, they do so relatively slowly. It takes years for market leaders to be replaced. Sequential declines in sales, no matter how small, may indicate the slow erosion of your customers' habitual repurchase behavior.

Use

In addition to getting customers to automate the purchase process, companies need to develop usage habits. In a B2B marketing example, habit formation revolves around the relationship. It is critical that a company be easy to work with, be easy to order from, and not create surprises. The person in purchasing is more likely to buy from the supplier that has an intuitive web site and one-click checkout than the competitor that has better prices but is hard to order from. Although FedEx advertises reliability, the convenience of its envelopes in the office makes FedEx use automatic. Convenience is integral to habit formation.

Travelers booking their own airline flights or hotel reservations have multiple online options. Airlines want customers to use their web sites to book flights, so they charge more for reservations made using a representative. However, the online marketplace is highly competitive with integrated travel sites such as Travelocity, Orbitz, or Expedia that search for flights across airlines and combine hotels and car rentals (services the airlines also offer).

Novice users might start at any of these sites based on advertising, web search, or reputation. As soon as they land on the home page, they begin learning the site's layout as they would in navigating a retail outlet. If the site is visually appealing, is intuitively designed, and provides good feedback, the user might not go anywhere else. But if the experience creates any level of frustration, habit formation will be inhibited.

In their pioneering work on automatic use, my colleagues Naresh Malhotra, Ph.D., from Georgia Tech, and Sung Kim, Ph.D., from the University of Wisconsin, Madison, have investigated the process of unconscious use with web sites and information systems.[2] Their research demonstrates that users go from intentional to unconscious, automatic use with multiple trips to a web site. The more experienced the user is, the less intention is involved in going to and using a particular web site.

---

[2] With Sridhar Narasimhan, Ph.D., also from Georgia Tech.

Building a web site that users visit repeatedly requires both an intuitive design and consistent reinforcement. Many web sites that are visually appealing fail to engage the customer on a behavioral level. Rich media, including video, can become a problem if it loads slowly or requires the user to download a player. Additionally, privacy and security concerns can prevent habitual use. Instead of putting security and privacy information on the home page, it is more effective to include assurances at the point where the user is required to enter personal information.

We can also extend the importance of habitual use to anyone in the buying center, including the purchaser, decider, and user. Bloomberg did a great job of selling terminals to brokerage houses by focusing on the end user, stockbrokers, while the competition was selling to the IT department. Cereal manufacturers create different messages for children (great taste with lots of crunch) than for the moms who typically make the purchase (less sugar, more vitamins).

Wireless carriers sell handsets with amazing capabilities, and broadband wireless networks can now deliver video, music, and a host of other data applications. But consumers don't use most of these applications. According to research from a major wireless carrier, customers who don't discover and use an application within the first 72 hours of getting the phone will probably never use it. The tricky part is that if the carriers try to get customers to use too many applications, the resulting complexity inhibits habit formation.

10

The Four Steps to Behavioral Marketing

We can break behavioral marketing into four critical stages: context, training, reinforcement, and cue. When these phases combine, they interlock to create the force of habit.

Context

The context of a habit is the why and where of behavior. Users can access music in many different ways, including listening to a radio, playing a CD, and using Internet radio, satellite, and MP3 players. One person might routinely listen to music using two, three, or even all of these methods, depending on context. You might wake up to radio music, listen to satellite radio driving to work, tune in to Internet radio when at your desk, and listen to your iPod when you go to the gym after work. Each of these choices is a habit within its own context.

For the wireless carrier and handset manufacturer to get you to listen to music on a cell phone, the company must either create a new context or replace habitual use in an existing context. This example illustrates the importance of thinking through all the steps that lead to habit formation. How does a customer put music on her cell phone? Does she have to download different software? Can she synch her phone's player to existing play lists? Does she have to pay again for music she already owns in another format?

But the biggest stumbling block to creating habitual music listening on a cell phone is not the technology, but the mental transformation that turns a handset into an MP3 player. The mental blocks of listening to music on a cell phone, such as battery life and audio quality, must be overcome.

The wireless industry gets very excited about the technology and services that they can cram into these tiny devices. As in many other high-tech industries, executives are enthralled with products that appeal to the executive mind, but these services are very unlikely to become habitual. For years, executives of my largest wireless client have been talking about owning "the third screen," with the TV and PC being the first two. They trumpet the ability to stream video and music to my handset. But I don't have a context for using my cell phone as a portable media center. I've been able to watch video on my cell phone for years, but I don't. After spending billions of dollars to enable these types of applications, their use remains insignificant. This doesn't mean they won't catch on, but if they do, it will be because customers develop a context for their use.

Erik Hanson, a media planner for Media Arts Lab, a subsidiary of advertising giant TBWA/Chiat/Day, has a phrase for this: the technology of least resistance. The less resistance is created for customers, the better the chance is that the technology will become part of everyday habits.

Training

When a context has been established, the behavior must be trained. This means that the behavior must be repeated sufficient times to develop automatic use within that context. Many people buy cars with built-in GPS or support services such as GM's OnStar. But using these capabilities rarely becomes habitual. A real estate agent or salesperson might use the navigation service weekly or possibly even daily. But most of us know where we're going most of the time, so the mere context of getting in the car might not trigger activation of the navigation system.

Also, the first uses of the service need to be reinforcing. If the navigation doesn't perform well on the first couple tries, its use cannot be integrated into habits. In addition, people have developed other habits for when they don't know how to get to their destination. Printing directions from MapQuest or Google maps is common, and a host of manufacturers sell portable GPS units that drivers can use on trips and in rental cars.

In working with one of my clients who was integrating GPS and mapping into a new cell phone, we came up with the idea of having traffic come up automatically when the user accessed the navigation function. The thought process is that users would routinely check this application before hitting the road, creating a reliable training mechanism.

By its very nature, habitual behavior is boring. We don't think about it. Although getting video on my cell phone is cool, I habitually use text messaging and email. The lure of sexy new applications should be tempered with the knowledge that companies are looking for relationships with their customers, not one-night stands.

Price becomes an essential issue during training. Use of cell phones is immediately reinforcing, but a large bill is punishment because it leads to less future use. Understanding that price needs to become a nonissue to develop repeat purchase behavior is critical. Whether it's a $6 latte or $60 video game, each product category creates its own range of affordability. Even if you are in the range of indifference, your brand promise has an implicit price associated with it. If you violate that price, the customer will keep the responsibility locked in executive mind review.

A nationwide effort is occurring to deceptively raise prices by breaking out fees separately from advertised prices. Clearly, this is effective because it has become so widespread. (I'm writing this section of the book from a hotel in Kansas City that tacked a $3 charge onto a room service bill under the category "Miscellaneous.") Be careful; when the threshold of indifference is crossed, the entire bill is up for review. Customers might decide they can live without premium cable channels, expensive wireless data plans, or their current bank.

By establishing a consistent context for product use, companies can begin to move intermittent behavior into habitual behavior through reinforcement. Training customers means making sure that specific behavior is being reinforced, either positively or negatively.

Reinforcement

Behaviors are repeated because they are reinforced. This statement explains why so much of our market research has yielded poor or false results. Reinforcement is anything that makes a behavior more likely to occur, but this process is ongoing, often on an unconscious level. Reinforcement can be inherent in the purchase, such as eating an ice cream cone on a hot summer day. But reinforcers can also be friendly service, quick checkout, and the people we're with.

The difference between reinforcement and rewards is that the former works with the habitual mind and the latter works with the executive mind. Reinforcement is the feedback mechanism that alters the firing patterns of neurons in the part of your brain that is learning unconsciously. Critical to this process is timing. A half-second delay can cause the executive mind to process a response, which can impede habitual learning.

Researchers attempting to develop an alert system to facilitate drivers' braking response time discovered it was most effective for a warning light to be visible for between 200th and 500th of a second. If the light stayed on longer than that, the conscious mind processed the information—increasing the time it takes a drive to react.

As mentioned, using a computer mouse is intuitive because the curser tracks seemingly simultaneously with the movement of the hand.

If a half-second delay occurs between the mouse moving and the cursor responding, learning is slow and frustrating.

In identifying the behaviors involved in discovery, purchase, and use, companies need to design corresponding reinforcements to guide habit formation.

Doug Rossier is a long-time client and the first manager to fully comprehend and work with me on developing a habit-based approach to product development and marketing. A long-time manager at a major wireless carrier, he was called in to discuss habits with a group responsible for loyalty. When the loyalty team explained that they were going to contact loyals (customer with three or more years uninterrupted service), they were surprised by his advice: "Don't!" While the loyalty group had the best of intentions, contacting these customers risks elevating the repurchase decision to the executive mind. Doug recommended that the group devise a series of "cookies" that could be used as periodic reinforcers and given to the company's best customers.

Cue

A cue activates a habit, similar to the first domino tumbling all the rest. A cue can be any stimulus associated with the context of the habit, including sights, sounds, smells, tastes, and even a touch. A combination of stimuli can also activate a response, such as the smells and sounds of a fast food restaurant cueing the script to order a burger and fries. Linking cues to behavior accelerates habit formation.

Research in Motion (RIM), a small Canadian company, entered the cutthroat world of wireless data in the late 1990s, going head-to-head with market leader Motorola. RIM's unique solution—a combination of a small swath of wireless spectrum, a handheld device, and middleware software—enabled mobile workers to receive their office email when they were away from their desks. At that time, other providers required the user to have a separate wireless email account. As more business processes came to depend on email, the RIM BlackBerry became essential.

However, what turned the BlackBerry into the CrackBerry (as users not-so-jokingly call it) is cue-based training. Mobility became the context for the BlackBerry, but the device's cueing mechanism leads to addiction. Emails are pushed to the BlackBerry so the user doesn't have to consciously think about retrieving them (the power of reducing steps). Upon arrival, the emails announce themselves with a tone or vibration, which becomes the cue. The power of the cue is that it triggers a behavior—checking the new email—which is immediately reinforced because the email has already been downloaded. The BlackBerry is also an excellent example of a device that works with the habitual mind so that the executive mind can focus on the task, evaluating and responding to emails.

11

Habit Maintenance

The most counterintuitive argument in this book is that companies don't want their customers to think about them, especially if the company is the market leader. If your customers are cruising on autopilot, leave them alone. If the repurchase behavior is dislodged from habit and raised to executive mind awareness, other brands might fall into consideration. Also, the customers might modify their purchase behavior. Let's look at a few scenarios in which this happens.

Any change to a product—including features, performance, appearance, price, or channel of distribution—risks moving a habit into executive mind review. I was surprised when my wife returned from shopping to replace our Ford Explorer that was totaled in an accident. She had really liked the Explorer, and I assumed she would get another. But she returned from the dealership disappointed, saying she didn't like the size of the new model. Of course, the larger size might have expanded the Explorer's appeal overall—I use this example to simply illustrate the point. Any change represents some level of risk.

However, not keeping the product updated can also disrupt habitual behavior. This is not a contradiction, but recognition that the brand promise is linked to maintaining the relationship in a changing marketplace. Not being able to keep an offer current is another form of breaking the brand promise. Hotel chains face tremendous costs to upgrade their properties, but if they don't, they face the slow erosion of customers. Kmart's neglect of its stores made the company look and feel outdated and cheap, and fall out of favor with customers and Wall

Street. Palm, previously viewed as a top innovator in handsets, faced criticism for keeping its form factor stable for too long—a couple of years. Tellingly, Palm hired former iPod lead designer Jon Rubinstein to help the company innovate.

Similarly, changing the underlying nature of the deal can dislodge existing habits, even if a company is sweetening the deal. Many sales promotions experience this drawback. Altering the nature of the deal interrupts automatic repurchase. The deal might become the new cue, as with coupons and annual sales.

Raising prices invariably risks elevating repurchase to executive review. Either stay below the range of indifference in price hikes or clearly articulate the reason for increase. Automobile companies were able to raise their prices for years by extending the payment plan thus keeping monthly payments the same. Conversely, the electronics industry faces relentless downward pressure on pricing. Branding can help make a product less sensitive to pricing pressures.

Schedules of Reinforcement

One other area of reinforcement is worth expanding. In my conversation with Karen Pryor, she discussed a problem with her clicker training web site. She was disappointed in sales and commented, "I had them build in a variable reinforcement schedule, but it doesn't seem to be working."

Variable reinforcement, reinforcing behaviors sporadically instead of every time they are performed, leads to behaviors that are more persistent and reliable. But companies must deliver on the brand promise every time. By reconciling these two principles, companies have an opportunity to create customer loyalty. Customer satisfaction research indicates that the only time a correlation exists between a satisfaction measure and repurchase is when a customer reports being delighted. Delight comes from being surprised, typically from receiving something unexpected or something more. New

Orleans has a word for that little something extra that a merchant drops in with a purchase: a *lagniappe*.

If companies give a *lagniappe* with every transaction, it quickly becomes an expectation and fails to create delight. However, if that little something extra is put on a variable schedule of reinforcement, customers' habits will be powerfully shaped toward persistent repurchase.

12

The Force of Habits:
The Double-Edged Sword

Although capturing customers' habits can lead to long-term profitable relationships, doing so requires changing the habits of the organization. The inertia of an individual customer's habit is nothing compared to that of a large company. Not only can the organizational structure (including policies, procedures, and processes) bog down offers designed to be habitual, but the behavior (habits) of individual employees can as well.

If market managers have been using customer satisfaction measures to grade employees, evaluate stores, and report to their bosses, they will experience tremendous resistance to change to a more meaningful metric. A product designer might create an intuitive interface based on a vision of habit formation, but product developers or product managers might reflexively add the bells and whistles that adorn all the company's other products. And even if the product vision survives development and commercialization, the advertising manager will probably show little interest in figuring out what the habit-forming message should be.

The solution is to treat your employees or coworkers like dogs. Reinforce those behaviors that incrementally lead to bringing habit-forming products and services to the marketplace. Add new metrics. Change the context of the decision-making process. Figure out what cookies work best in your organization and when to install buzzers.

Unfortunately, organizational structures can inadvertently create complexities that the customer must navigate. When I took my father to a cancer clinic for treatment, I was appalled to see the receptionist hand him a clipboard with eight pages of forms that needed to be filled out. Frustrated, I asked the receptionist why this information wasn't transmitted from the referring physician and why so many forms existed. Her reply was dismissive. "Each department creates its own forms." A quick review of the paperwork showed that 80% of each form asked for the same information. Although it would have been easy to make a single form that could be copied and distributed, the clinic allowed its organizational structure to dictate a complex and time-consuming process for its clients.

Large companies often experience this problem when employees far removed from customers make decisions that can add layers of complexity. By prioritizing habit formation, companies will objectively see the need to streamline these processes.

Conclusion

Every marketplace is controlled by the habits of its customers. Incumbents maintain their position only as long as their customers maintain their habitual behavior. New entrants can only succeed if they supplant the entrenched unconscious behavior of one or more existing segments or by creating new habits thus creating new markets.

Some of our most entrenched habits are undergoing profound transformations. We no longer read the daily paper religiously (as the stock price of most dailies attest). Cell phones have replaced landline phones for millions, and a new generation views email as old-fashioned. Even carbonated beverage sales are experiencing a persistent 2% annual decline.

Yet each of these major shifts, which seem so revolutionary, occurred over time as neural circuits in the habitual mind became primed to reach for the cell phone instead of a landline or a bottle of water instead of a soda. The Internet makes it possible for companies like YouTube, MySpace, and Facebook to achieve billion dollar capitalizations in a matter of months, but their success is inexorably linked to the power of social networks to create new habits.

Hopefully this book has made the case for a major overhaul of marketing based on a better understanding of how our brains work. But the true value of *Habit* will come from managers rethinking their approach to creating and maintaining relationships with their customers. By understanding how to design products, choose distribution channels, set prices, and craft messages for both the habitual as well as the executive minds, it is possible to create unconscious customer loyalty—the most important asset any company can own.

INDEX

FT Press

FINANCIAL TIMES

In an increasingly competitive world, it is quality
of thinking that gives an edge—an idea that opens new
doors, a technique that solves a problem, or an insight
that simply helps make sense of it all.

We work with leading authors in the various arenas
of business and finance to bring cutting-edge thinking
and best-learning practices to a global market.

It is our goal to create world-class print publications
and electronic products that give readers
knowledge and understanding that can then be
applied, whether studying or at work.

To find out more about our business
products, you can visit us at www.ftpress.com.